BRINGING HOME THE WEDDING
HANDBOOK

Elisa Gaye Wagoner

A Do-It-Yourself Handbook
for Home and Out-of-Door Weddings

First Edition

Edited by:
Amy Ammons Garza

Cover Illustration and design by:
Doreyl Ammons Cain

Inside Illustrations by:
Elisa G. Wagoner

PUBLISHED BY:

Ammons Communications, LTD.
64 Windsong Lane, Whittier, NC 28789
Phone & Fax 1-828-631-9203

Library of Congress Catalog Card Number: 98-68531

ISBN: 0-9651232-5-1

Contents

Acknowledgements

I wish to acknowledge all helping hands seen and unseen, the God Spirit within and without who moves my hand, mind and soul.

A special thanks to Julie Eckes, Larry T. Reida and Amy Ammons Garza, who with wisdom and grace edited "Bringing Home The Wedding". A warm thank you to dear friends and family for their love, encouragement and comments on this project.

Love and gratitude; to my wonderful daughters, Aimee' Danielle, Melody Dawn and Gaebrielle Lisette for devoting long hours modeling my fashions before the camera and on the runway, and to my son Simon Donald.

And thanks Mom and Dad for nurturing within me your great love for home, family and woodland gardens.

Author's Note: *As a child I became a protégée of my seamstress mother. When I sewed a seam wrong, she asked me to take the seam out and do it again - over and over again. At this very young age, it grew to be frustrating. "It's the details, step by step, that create your fashion," she would tell me.*

This early introduction by my mother into the art of clothing design and construction was the best education I could have ever received. The more I learned, the more I wanted to learn. I studied, receiving a fine arts degree; I lived abroad, studying and working as a commercial artist, public relations professional, wardrobe mistress, and freelance writer/artist/photographer. Through this wide-angle view of the world came my appreciation for the romantics and old world perfection, which, in turn developed into my fashion preference. Designing and producing clothing for the romantic spirit swept me into sales and speciality boutiques. With the subsequent success of this venture, I eventually opened my own business, Elisa Gaye Designer Boutique in Waynesville, NC. Currently, my shop - featuring original fashions, patterns and this book - is being designed for the internet.

Many years of study and work went into the pages of this book. But I have come full circle...back to my mother's words: "It's the details, step by step, that create...." May you, the readers of my book, reap the benefits of her wisdom.

Elisa Gaye Wagoner

Chapter 1

BRINGING HOME THE WEDDING

"There is no place more delightful than home"
Marcus Tullius Cicero 106-43 B.C.

Grassroots America is bringing home the wedding. Many brides and grooms across the country have abandoned the formal wedding fuss in favor of a simply elegant wedding in the home, out-of-doors or "home away from home" (the ancestral home, a historic home site, or a romantic seaside inn) Home and out-of-door weddings have appeal for first and second time brides and grooms who may already be financing their educations or investing in new careers or a house. Some couples have discovered there is unnecessary stress in hosting a large Hollywood production style wedding. Your wedding can be a personalized and manageable celebration on your terms with careful and creative planning. The possibilities are unlimited, your garden for example; can be a beautiful arboretum, botanical or winter garden, a municipal or national park. Your Chamber of Commerce, Town Hall, Historical Society and Universities have an abundance of possibilities waiting to host your wedding. Bringing Home The Wedding is a handbook that shows you, step-by-step how to plan the wedding ceremony and reception of your dreams within your budget, without stress or fuss.

The Budget check list in Chapter 2 is a list of goods and services available for your wedding. Establish your budget, select items from the Budget Check List that you want to include in your wedding, then total the cost. Fine tune the list until it meets your budget. A little creativity and imagination will help you achieve some beautiful effects at a low cost. Chapter 6 illustrates step-by-step instructions on how to create eight beautiful wedding projects.

Weddings are made up of two parts, the ceremony and the reception, which can all take place at home or your out-of-doors site. Or a house of worship ceremony can be followed by a reception at home, out-of-doors or at a "home away from home." The clergy or civil officiant can be brought in to perform the wedding ceremony at your chosen wedding site. A step-by-step plan in Chapter 4 "Wedding Ceremony" lists three ceremony styles to choose from. Chapter 5, Wedding Reception, gives step-by-step instructions for a self-catered wedding, organizing a commercially catered wedding and a Beautiful Wedding under $2000.

Chapters 7, 8 and 9 plan your reception with a choice of 5 wedding menus and 35 tested recipes, information on the art of toasting, serving instruction for wine, coffee and tea to a gathering. Garden Wedding Attire is detailed in Chapter 3 for bride and groom. Helpful information and check lists remind you when to attend to invitations, flowers, music, photography and transportation.

Chapter 2

GETTING STARTED ON YOUR WEDDING

ESTABLISH PRIORITIES

Some couples will assume total expense for their wedding while other couples will share the expense with their parents, in which case, consulting with family members is necessary. Weddings in the United States can cost anywhere from $18,000 to $60,000 +. It's wise to remember that money spent on a very large wedding would go a long way toward a home mortgage or business. Again, it is your choice to do what is comfortable for you and your budget.

Your greatest wedding expense is the wedding reception; the more guests, the greater the cost. Set your budget then list the "absolute must guests" that you want to attend your wedding. This will require diplomacy and patience when working with your families on the guest list. If the final guest list outweighs your budget, then make adjustments on the style of wedding reception; for example, an elegant dessert and coffee buffet after the ceremony. Refer to chapter 5, Wedding Menus, lists 5 menus, 35 tested recipes.

SET THE BUDGET

The Budget Check List will give you an idea how much your wedding will cost based upon the goods and services you buy. Read *Bringing Home The Wedding* first so that you understand the options available to you in planning your event. Check which goods and services apply to the style wedding you want, then telephone the suppliers for estimates and pencil in the figures under the "estimate" column. Prices will vary considerably so shop around to get good value for a good price. Ask friends and family for recommendations. Establish with each supplier by telephone if they are available on your wedding date. When you have firmed up your plan enter the figures under total cost column and add up the total wedding expense. Sign a contract with the suppliers of goods and services detailing every item. Remember weddings have a way of taking a life of their own, so do your homework and closely monitor your priorities and budget.

BUDGET CHECK LIST:

WEDDING RECEPTION

Item	Estimate	Total cost
Self-Catered Wedding Reception		
Cost per person from menu times total guests ...	$	$
Wine	$	$
Champagne	$	$
Liquor	$	$
Liquor license	$	$
Wedding cake	$	$
Staff:		
Food preparation	$	$
Serving	$	$
Bartending	$	$
Valet Parking	$	$
Equipment rental:		
Tent	$	$
Canopy	$	$
Cutlery	$	$
China	$	$
Stemware	$	$
Glasses	$	$
Linens	$	$
Tables	$	$
Chairs	$	$
Coffee maker	$	$
Tea pots	$	$
Chafing dish	$	$
Warming table	$	$
Ice chest	$	$
Large grill	$	$
Gazebo	$	$
Fountain	$	$
Plants	$	$
Flowers	$	$
Landscape services	$	$
Electrical	$	$
Special lighting	$	$
Plumbing	$	$
Portable commode	$	$
Equipment setup, tear down, clean up	$	$
TOTAL	$	$

Item		Estimate	Total Cost
Sew-It-Yourself Wedding Accessories			
Table cloths	....	$	$
Chair cushions	....	$	$
Placemats	....	$	$
Napkins	....	$	$
	TOTAL	$	$

Item		Estimate	Total Cost
Commercially Catered Reception			
Cost per person from menu	....	$	$
Fees and gratuities	....	$	$
Wine	....	$	$
Champagne	....	$	$
Open Bar	....	$	$
Corkage fee	....	$	$
Liquor license	....	$	$
Wedding cake	....	$	$
Valet parking	....	$	$
Bartending	....	$	$
Food serving	....	$	$
Wedding cake cutting and serving	....	$	$
Valet parking	....	$	$
Clean up	....	$	$
Equipment rental			
Tent	....	$	$
Canopy	....	$	$
Cutlery	....	$	$
China	....	$	$
Stemware	....	$	$
Glasses	....	$	$
Linens	....	$	$
Tables	....	$	$
Chairs	....	$	$
Coffee maker	....	$	$
Tea pot	....	$	$
Chafing dish	....	$	$
Warming table	....	$	$
Ice chest	....	$	$
Large grill	....	$	$
Gazebo	....	$	$
Fountain	....	$	$
Plants	....	$	$

Landscape services	$	$
Electrical	$	$
Special lighting	$	$
Plumbing	$	$
Portable commode	$	$
Equipment set up, tear down, clean up	$	$
TOTAL	$	$

Item	Under $2000	Your Cost
A Beautiful Wedding under $2000	(25 guests)	(___ guests)
CEREMONY (in the garden)		
Clergy	$ 125.00	$
Live Music	$ 350.00	$
Photographer	$ 550.00	$
Flowers (farmers market and contributions from friend's gardens)	$ 150.00	$
Invitations (computer generated)	$ .00	$
email/fax	$ .00	$
Brides dress and accessories (cost of fabric, pattern, seamstress and accessories)	$ 185.00	$
Grooms attire (dry cleaning)	$ 20.00	$
Marriage license	$ 40.00	$
Medical requirements	$ .00	$
RECEPTION (in the garden)		
Volunteers to prepare and serve buffet	$ .00	$
Ingredients cost for buffet	$ 375.00	$
Champagne	$ 50.00	$
Coffee and non alcoholic beverage	$ 25.00	$
Stemware with wine/champagne purchase	$ .00	$
Paper napkins	$ 2.50	$
Plates (personal and borrowed)	$ .00	$
Coffee cups (personal and borrowed)	$ .00	$
Cutlery (personal and borrowed)	$ .00	$
Balloons	$ 3.50	$
Twinkle lights (some borrowed, some new)	$ 5.75	$
Equipment rental		
Canopy (10' x 10')	$ 40.00	$
Folding table	$ 10.00	$
Folding chairs	$ 6.25	$
Coffee urn	$ 18.00	$
Industrial chafing dish	$ 20.00	$
TOTAL	$ 1976.00	$

Item	Estimate	Total Cost
Ceremony: House of Worship/ Wedding Chapel		
Fees and Gratuities	$	$
Clergy	$	$
Organist	$	$
Musicians	$	$
Soloist	$	$
Custodial	$	$
Wedding rings	$	$
TOTAL	$	$

Item	Estimate	Total Cost
Ceremony in the Home and Garden		
Clergy/Civil officiant	$	$
Musicians	$	$
Soloist	$	$
Ceremony equipment leasing		
Candelabras	$	$
Kneeling benches	$	$
Wedding arches	$	$
Canopy	$	$
Gazebo, rose trellis	$	$
Vases	$	$
Equipment set up, tear down, clean up	$	$
Wedding rings	$	$
TOTAL	$	$

Item	Estimate	Cost
Bride's Attire		
Wedding dress	$	$
Bride's Accessories:		
Slip	$	$
Panties	$	$
Bra	$	$
Stockings	$	$
Shoes	$	$
Hat	$	$
Gloves	$	$
Handbag	$	$
Jewelry	$	$
Personal Care		
Massage	$	$
Day at the spa	$	$

	Estimate	Cost
Hair care	$	$
Cosmetics	$	$
Nail care	$	$
Fragrance	$	$
TOTAL	$	$

Item	Estimate	Cost
Groom's Attire		
Tuxedo	$	$
Shirt	$	$
Tie	$	$
Under shirt	$	$
Shorts	$	$
Shoes	$	$
Socks	$	$
Jewelry	$	$
Personal Care	$	$
Massage	$	$
Hair care	$	$
Manicure	$	$
Personal wardrobe dry cleaning	$	$
TOTAL	$	$

Item	Estimate	Cost
Gifts for Bridal Party		
Bridal Attendants	$	$
Groomsmen	$	$
TOTAL	$	$

Item	Estimate	Cost
Rest and Recreation For Couple		
Candlelight dinners	$	$
Trips to the Spa	$	$
Weekend retreats	$	$
Entertaining out of town guests	$	$
TOTAL	$	$

Item	Estimate	Total Cost
Flowers or Plants		
Bride's bouquet	$	$
Bride's hair piece	$	$
Mothers	$	$
Attendants	$	$

Groom	$	$
Groomsmen	$	$
Ceremony site	$	$
Reception site	$	$
TOTAL	$	$

Item	Estimate	Cost
Photography		
Photographer	$	$
Videographer	$	$
Disposable cameras	$	$
TOTAL	$	$

Item	Estimate	Cost
Music		
Live music	$	$
Disc jockey	$	$
Personal sound system	$	$
TOTAL	$	$

Item	Estimate	Cost
Transportation		
Personal and vehicle liability insurance	$	$
Horse, carriage, coachman	$	$
Liability Insurance	$	$
Leased vehicles		
Limousine	$	$
Vintage cars	$	$
Taxi	$	$
TOTAL	$	$

PRIORITY CALENDAR:

Whether your wedding is scheduled in a year or just a few months away, the event can be coordinated with a minimum fuss by making use of the Priority Calendar. This method will provide you with a visible means to track your progress and act as a reminder when the next item needs your attention. Pencil into the blank calendar format; the year, month, and number each day in the month. Make entries for the task that needs your attention on the lines for each day of the month. Should you need more than six Priority Calendars, photo copy additional sheets before entering your data.

PRIORITY CALANDER

(MONTH)_____   (YEAR)_____

SUN	MON	TUE	WED	THURS	FRI	SAT

PRIORITY CALANDER

(MONTH)_____   (YEAR)_____

SUN	MON	TUE	WED	THURS	FRI	SAT

PRIORITY CALANDER

(MONTH)_____   (YEAR)_____

SUN	MON	TUE	WED	THURS	FRI	SAT

PRIORITY CALANDER

(MONTH)_____   (YEAR)_____

SUN	MON	TUE	WED	THURS	FRI	SAT

PRIORITY CALANDER

(MONTH)_____   (YEAR)_____

SUN	MON	TUE	WED	THURS	FRI	SAT

PRIORITY CALANDER

(MONTH)_____   (YEAR)_____

SUN	MON	TUE	WED	THURS	FRI	SAT

TIPS FOR A STRESS FREE WEDDING

1. A mother of the bride who coordinated the weddings of each of her three daughters states, "I created an artificial deadline one week in advance of the actual event. In doing so, I was able to enjoy all the dinner parties and out of town guests without being too preoccupied about the wedding."

2. After you have decided upon a wedding date, theme, ceremony and reception site, write a lighthearted newsletter. Mail, fax or email it to out-of-town guests well in advance of the wedding date so that they can make arrangements for time off work and travel plans.

3. Compile a "Task List" of details that need to be accomplished and when it must be done.
   * Delegate tasks to friends and family volunteer "team" members.
   * Assign a captain to the "team" of volunteers to oversee the progress.
   * Meet over lunch or dinner periodically to discuss development of the tasks.
   * Send a "Task Report" to all team members, tracking progress of their assignments.
   List names, phone number, pager number and "task" of each team member.

4. The unforseen always happens, anticipate this and be calm, it will all work out. Step back often, take a deep breath, watch the proceedings and enjoy it, it's your party!

5. Out of Town Guests: Create a Wedding Guest Package for out of town guests with phone numbers of contact persons as you may not be available when they arrive. Include a map of wedding activity locations. Provide a list of accommodations in close proximity to the wedding activities in an affordable price range and names of possible baby sitters. Suggest the best mode of transportation to your home town, highway route if they are driving or airline schedule and fees. Provide a folder of things to do while they are visiting, local attractions, shopping, leisure activities, maps and seasonal climate in your area.

6. Take time out to smell the roses! Plan frequent trips to the spa, gym and candlelight dinners with your partner.

RECENT HOME AND OUT-OF-DOOR WEDDINGS:

My daughter and son-in-law **Gaebrielle and James**, married on the first day of winter, under a sanctuary of century old sycamore trees at their home in Southern California. Rose petals and long stem roses adorned the garden where their carefully scripted vows were exchanged. With 3000 miles between us, Gaebrielle and I co-designed (with the use of a fax machine) her German Renaissance gown in white shimmer velvet, detailed in ermine fur and soutache trim. To complete the ensemble, I created a long violet, velvet, satin-lined cape. James wore a wonderful Baroque period costume that he rented from a theatre company and his own riding boots, setting a poetic mood for these two literary devotees. Harpist and flautist played while family and friends toasted the union of this couple at a delightful medieval feast.

My friends **Gail and Henry** are horticulturists, so planning a garden wedding on the grounds of his mothers home in North Carolina was a lasting contribution of their combined creativity, not to mention, a marvellous photo opportunity. Officiated by their family minister, they exchanged vows in the garden, under the rose arbour. Gail wore a tea length long-sleeved gown with a high Victorian collar in ecru lace. Henry wore a sports jacket and light slacks. A catered beef Bar-B-Q in the garden was attended by family and friends while their favorite Bluegrass band played.

Judith and Tom's love for dancing influenced the style of their garden wedding and her dress. I designed her retro's 1930's two-piece-satin-lined dress with tulip skirt in white Venice lace, with long streamers at the back. Tom wore a '30 style black suit with a fedora. They exchanged vows in a gazebo by a stream in the orchard at Judith's ancestral home. A rented dance floor in the orchard was surrounded by pretty chairs and tables in calico, decorated by Judith. Guests enjoyed a garden buffet prepared by family, after which bride and groom danced with friends and family to a live band (well into the next day, so I'm told).

Deidra and Michael chose wildflowers and butterflies as a theme for their late summer garden wedding back home in Oregon. Wild flowers grown by family in Oregon, formed her bouquet, headpiece and decorations for church and garden celebration. Deirdra chose my cap sleeved, mid-calf length, princess style dress with very low back and scoop neckline in white embroidered eyelet. The bodice, detailed with Venice lace, tucks, pintucks and tiny pearl buttons, was accented with a white satin sash, tied at the back. She wore a wide brim hat adorned with wildflowers. Her groom wore a rented black tux. After a church ceremony, live butterflies were released by guests outside the church, to symbolize joining together two people into a new life. A traditional pig roast celebration in the garden was coordinated and catered by family and friends.

Mary Jo and John were financing a new business, and an antique home in Ontario Canada. Mary Jo wore a vintage floor length gown in white satin with drop waist, long sleeves and sweetheart neckline embroidered with pearls and sequins. John and his groomsmen wore rented black tuxedos. After a church wedding one block away, the bride, groom, guests and musicians promenaded (European style) to the couples' home where they celebrated on the verandah, in the garden and drawing room. Rented chairs, tables and a climate controlled tent, extended the social space and protected the gathering from the hot August sun. A reception of hors d'oeuvres and champagne was prepared in advance by Mary Jo, John and friends. Musicians played while guests danced in the garden, under the stars.

Chapter 3

WEDDING ATTIRE

BRIDAL ATTIRE:

Once you have established your wedding theme, select the dress of your dreams. Keep in mind which style looks and feels best on your figure. Set your budget for bridal gown, shoes, headpiece, gloves, intimate apparel and jewelry. Decide on your hairstyle, makeup, nails and fragrance well before the wedding so that the total effect is consistent. You have the option of shopping at a salon, having your dress designed, made by a seamstress or wearing a vintage wedding dress.

Bridal Salon

When making your selection from a sample gown that you have tried on, record the model number, price, description of the style, detailing and the fabric. Ask what deposit is required and fees for alterations. Be sure that your measurements coincide with the manufacturers measurements for the size being ordered. Obtain the name and phone number of the store and sales person. Have your friend or your mother take a photo of you wearing the sample that you have selected. Bring a pair of shoes with you when you try on dresses (close to the color and style you will wear with your dress) Be certain your dress can be delivered by your wedding date. The company who manufactures the gown you have selected will wait until their quota is filled, (8 to 10 orders of that same design) before going into production. This is common practice and an efficient way to do business, but the bridal salon has no way of knowing when the quota has been filled. Assume nothing, keep in touch with the salon on the progress of your gown. Ask for and research the salon's references and Better Business rating.

Fashion Designer

To locate a fashion designer, contact the Chamber of Commerce in your area, craft guilds, telephone directory, or fabric stores. Phone for an appointment and ask to see samples and photographs of the designers work. If their styles are compatible with the idea you have in mind for your dress, ask if they will work with you in co-creating your dress. Bring photos from magazine illustrating the style you want. Be certain your dress can be completed before your wedding date. Ask the designer for sample fabric (to match up with your accessories). Obtain a breakdown of the fees, deposit required, when the first fitting will be scheduled and when the garment will be completed. Bring your shoes to the fitting, head piece and accessories. It is wise to decide upon a hair style that compliments your dress and headpiece well before the wedding.

A designer is the ideal solution for difficult to fit sizes or a bride with very definite style ideas. For Mina, one of my Rubenesque brides, I designed a retro's 1960 trapeze dress in white embroidered Venice lace with elbow length cape sleeves. The low sweetheart neckline detailed with appliques, pearls and sequins, disclosed her wonderful cleavage (Rubens would be pleased!) A sweeping mid-calf hem at the front, curved down to brush the floor in a mock train.

Connie, a tall slender redhead was married in a retro 1940's three-piece suit I designed in white silk shantung. Her long sleeve fitted jacket, detailed with wide shawl collar and bustled peblem, was worn with a knee length straight skirt with a low cut white satin camisole. I found a lovely wide brim hat for her in white straw with a black crown; she accessorised with black and white spectator shoes, clutch and white gloves. I heard later that she turned heads, and enjoyed every minute of it.

Seamstress

Consult your yellow pages, classified ads, fabric stores and friends for the names and phone numbers of seamstresses. Ask to see samples or photos of the seamstress wedding dresses. Obtain references and ask if he/she can complete the dress before your wedding date. Purchase a commercial pattern for a bridal dress at your local fabric store. Most sales assistants in fabric stores are very knowledgeable and will help you select the fabric and necessary notions for your dress. If you want to be sure the style you select looks well on you before purchasing expensive fabric, sew a sample in cheap cotton (or have a friend or relative help you). If the style doesn't work for you, purchase another pattern in a different style and make that one up in cotton. The only thing that you've lost is the cost of a pattern and cotton.

Bridal Attire Suggestions

Informal
DRESS: Short, medium, long or mini; sheath, princess, empire seaming or drop waist; flared at the hem or fitted; scoop, square or 'V' neck, low back or backless; long, 3/4, short sleeve or sleeveless.
FABRIC: Tencel, Charmuese, Double Georgette, Polyester, Double Crepe, Sand Washed Silk, Shantung, Linen, Dotted Swiss or Embroidered Eyelet.
COLOR: White, oyster, pastels, vibrant solids or muted prints.
SUIT: Long or short skirt, straight, 'A' line or flared skirt, with a fitted or cropped jacket. Sheath or 'A' line dress with matching jacket.

FABRIC: Polyester/Rayon Linen, Faille Brocade, Cotton/Polyester Jacquard.

PANT DRESS: Same basic styles as dress, short or long, straight or palazzo pant. Depending on the fabric you choose, the addition of an over skirt will create a exotic look and extend the life of the garment.

FABRIC: Tencel, Sand-Washed Silk, Polyester Peau Satin, Polyester/Rayon Linen.

COLOR: White, oyster, pastels, dramatic solids or muted prints.

GLOVES: Short lace or cotton glove (or romantic fingerless glove with cotton blend dress).

HEADPIECE: A wide brim hat garnished with silk flowers on the inside brim or under side of the brim. A smart little "Pill Box" hat with over-sized single flower to the right with a discreet chin veil. I recommend wearing fresh flowers in season in your hair whenever possible. Whether your hair is long or short, the effect is always alluring. Try securing a flower or two to your comb or use bobbie pins to get the feel of a poetic look. Position the flower to the right side of your face as an accent on hair upswept, cascading or gathered at the back. A garland of delicate flowers on the crown or at the nape of the neck can be oh! so provocative. Refer to Chapter 13 "Flowers" for more illustrations and instructions on creating your floral head piece.

SHOES: Retro shoes with blocky heels, sandal strap, pump or attractive flat heel shoe. Remember, you will be on your feet all day and comfort is an absolute must! Wear your wedding shoes at home to break them in. Pull a pair of old socks over them to keep them from being marked.

Formal

DRESS: A floor length dress with or without

a train, styled with a drop waist, princess or empire seaming. The dress can be an elegant sheath or flared at the hem, sleeveless or with long or short sleeves. Choose a neckline that suits you; a high or low scoop, 'V' or square neckline.

FABRIC: Polyester, Peau Satin, Double Georgette, 100% Silk, Embroidered Organza, Chiffon, Shimmer Velvet, Velvet or Venice Lace.

COLOR: White, oyster, pastels or a muted print.

HEADPIECE: Chapel or cathedral veil, silk or fresh flower garland in the hair (see headpiece, informal bridal wear, above). Refer to Chapter 13 "Flowers" for illustrations and details on creating your own floral headpiece.

GLOVES: Long satin gloves with short sleeve and sleeveless dress, short gloves with long sleeve gown.

SHOES: Retro styles or a pump with a low heel; comfort an absolute must!

GROOM'S ATTIRE:

Unless you plan to wear a tuxedo for other social occasions, it makes sense to rent your tuxedo. Rental runs anywhere from $60 to $150 dollars, including shoes. If you or your groomsmen are renting tuxedos, ask for package discounts. Make tuxedo reservations well in advance of your wedding, and schedule your fittings at that time.

If your wedding theme is unique, such as retro 1920's, medieval or provincial, research costume rental companies or theatre companies for suitable attire. Consider having a designer or seamstress make the Groom's theme wedding costume.

For the informal wedding it is perfectly acceptable for groom and groomsmen to wear their own suit and shoes, preferably black or dark in color with white, striped or colored shirt and suitable tie. The relaxed look of a blazer with coordinating trousers with white, colored or textured shirt and tie, is a clean look for the informal wedding. For country and western wedding try a denim sports coat or vest with coordinating trousers, striped shirt, tie and boots.

CHECK LIST FOR WEDDING ATTIRE

Bridal Salon:
Record the following information on your wedding dress contract. Assume nothing; keep in touch with the salon on the progress of your dress.
Confirm that garment will be completed by your date _____
Order date _____ Delivery date _____
Model number _____ Fabric choice _____
Description of the style _____
Bring shoes to wear when trying on dresses _____ Photo of dress purchased_____
First fitting date (bring headpiece/accessories) _____
Bridal salon _____
Address _____ Phone _____
Sales assistant _____
Total cost _____ Deposit _____ Payment schedule including alterations _____
Cancellation policy _____

* Note: Be certain that your measurements coincide with the manufacturers measurements for the size being ordered to avoid excessive alteration fees.

Bust _____ Waist _____

Hip _____ Back waist length _____

Waist to hem _____

Fashion Designer:
Ask to see samples and photographs of the designers work. Will the designer work with you in co-creating your dress? Bring photos from magazine illustrating the style you want. Record the following data on your contract or order form. Assume nothing; keep in touch with your designer on the progress of your dress.

Confirm that garment will be complete before your date _____
Order date _____ Delivery date _____
Model number _____ Fabric sample _____
Description of the style _____
_____
First fitting date (bring shoes/head piece/accessories) _____
Company name _____
Address _____
Designers name _____ Phone _____
Total cost _____ Deposit _____ Payment schedule including alterations _____
Cancellation policy _____

Seamstress:

Purchase and bring the wedding dress pattern and fabric and make an appointment with the seamstress. Ask to see samples or photos of wedding dresses made by the seamstress. Request references. Record the following information on your contract or order form when you secure the services of your seamstress. Assume nothing; keep in touch with your seamstress on the progress of your dress.

Confirm that the garment will be completed before your wedding date _____

Order date _____ Delivery date _____

Pattern company and number _____ Fabric sample _____

Describe in detail any changes made to style _____

First fitting (bring shoes, head piece and accessories) _____

Company name _____

Seamstress name _____

Address _____ Phone number _____

Authorized signature _____

Total cost _____ Deposit _____ Payment schedule including alterations _____

Cancellation policy _____

Groom's Attire:

Detail tuxedo(s) and all accessories rented in your contract. Reconfirm that everything will be available for the wedding date. Rent attire at least two to five month prior to the wedding and schedule fitting(s) at this time.

Confirm tuxedo (or theme attire) and accessories available before your date _____

Order date _____ Delivery date _____

Model number _____ Color _____

Detail style description _____

Shirt _____Tie _____ Vest _____

Belt/suspenders/cummerbund _____

Socks _____ Shoes _____

Fitting date _____

Company name _____

Address _____ Phone _____

Sales assistant _____

Authorized signature _____

Total cost _____ Deposit _____ Payment schedule including alterations _____

Cancellation policy _____

*Dry clean personal tuxedo _____ suit _____ accessories _____

Notes for wedding apparel

Chapter 4

YOUR WEDDING:

HOME AND OUT-OF-DOOR WEDDING

> *"Beneath the orchard's spreading apple blossoms, guests gather while the family cleric officiates the wedding ceremony. Blossoms fall like confetti. A colorful tent on the lawn offers shelter for guests who toast the newlyweds, while a dear friend's camera captures memories for their tomorrows. Flowers cut from grandmother's garden are arranged in porcelain pitchers adding charm to the catered buffet on the verandah. Music from a live ensemble mingles with the fragrance of lilac. A handmade tablecloth covers a table where the bride and groom stand ready to cut the wedding cake. What bliss!"*

Weddings usually consist of two parts, the ceremony and the reception. Both can take place at one site (your home), or at two locations: a ceremony at a house of worship and reception at your home. The wedding of your dreams may be as close as your own home, ancestral home or the home of dear friends or perhaps a mountain top country inn. A cleric or civil officiant can be brought in to perform your wedding ceremony. Be sure to book their services well in advance of your wedding date to avoid disappointment. Establish all fees, gratuities and travel expenses well in advance for those whose services you require for your wedding.

Plan your wedding to suit your budget, lifestyle, facilities and the number of guests you have invited. Regard interior and exterior as potential social spaces; open them up and let the party move to and from the home and garden. Consider storing some excess home furniture to free up space so guests can circulate during the festivities. For the ceremony, position yourselves and the cleric/civil officiant so you will be visible to your guests; elevated on the stairs, a gazebo, under a canopy or wedding arch. For a small wedding consider catering the event yourself with the help of "team" volunteers. For a larger wedding hire a limited or full service catering company. Refer to Chapter 5, Wedding Reception.

HOSTING YOUR WEDDING AT LEASED OR REMOTE FACILITIES

The Great Smoky Mountain National Park in Tennessee was the wedding site of choice for a Maryland couple who met there while hiking. If your dream is to be wed at the seaside, a mountaintop or desert, an equipment rental company can provide the comforts of home with attractive tents, food preparation, warming and serving equipment. An electrical generator will power your lighting, heating, cooling and sound system needs. A portable commode, dance floor and whatever else your heart desires, can be realized. It is always useful to have the names and phone numbers of a reliable handyman, electrician, plumber and carpenter to fine tune your wedding preparations. A memorable occasion can be achieved with some creative planning and a little flexibility. Consult with your Chamber of Commerce, Town Hall, Historical Society or university; they have some surprising and delightful possibilities for your wedding. Inquire what is legally required in the region where you plan to be married; marriage license, blood tests, medical, birth certificates.

PREPARING THE HOME AND OUT-OF-DOOR SPACE

When organizing your seasonal home and garden cleaning and maintenance, keep in mind the interior and exterior spaces you plan to use for your wedding. Ensure that all electrical, plumbing and appliances are in good working order. Arrange to have furniture, carpets, floors, windows, drapes and curtains cleaned and any painting and repairs done well in advance of the wedding date. Keep a pad and pencil handy to jot down notes of things-to-do. Consider storing some bulky pieces of furniture during the wedding celebration to facilitate a flow of traffic around your serving stations. If storage units are not close by, furniture can be stored in a leased truck and parked nearby, out of sight. Be sure there is an adequate supply of towels, soap and toilet tissue. Plan your annual and perennial planting so that your gardens will be in full bloom on your wedding day. Add plants, hanging flower baskets, benches, a fountain or gazebo. Consider where a canopy, awning or tent can be placed to expand your social space and to act as shelter from weather. If you plan live music or a dance band you may want to lease a dance floor and some sound equipment. Tidy up the grounds and store tools and machinery in the garden shed away from sight. Plan where guests will park their car. Remember to delegate duties to "team" members. This is your party, relax and enjoy it!

DECORATING THE WEDDING SITE

Canopy, Awning and Tent:
Expand your social space and shelter guests and food from exposure to the weather with a canopy, awning or tent. Today, tents are climate controlled, lighted, have cathedral ceilings and roll up-and-down walls with windows. They invite guests to drift in and out at will. You can plan one large tent or a series of pretty little canopies which function for dancing, dining and as serving stations. An equipment leasing company will help you calculate the size tent you need based upon the number of guests and style of function. An estimate commonly used is, twelve square feet per person for a sit down affair. For example: one 20' x 20' tent will accommodate a sit down dinner for 30 persons, or a buffet for 36 persons, or a stand up cocktail reception for 46 persons. Sone leasing companies will set up and tear down equipment. If possible, have the grass cut and set up the tent a day or two before the event if it should rain, so that the ground will be dry for the wedding day. Lighting punk sticks or citronella candles will keep the insect population down. Rented plants, trees, hanging flowering plants, stage, dance floor and fountain will define social spaces and create an attractive promenade path.

Sew- It-Yourself Wedding Decorations:

Decorate the reception tables and wedding cake table with imaginative treatments: tailored or flounced table cloth sets with matching napkins, place mats and chair cushions. For an elegant effect, try swags drawn up with jabots on your reception or wedding cake table. Complete the effect with some fancy folded napkins. Sewing instructions are found in Chapter 6.

Special Effect Lighting:

Shrubs and medium size trees in the garden can be strung with twinkle lights, adding a gala effect and illuminating the social spaces. Lights will also call attention to focal points, lead the way to washroom facilities and prevent guests from tripping on obstacles, such as tent support ropes. Colored paper lantern groupings can define social spaces and add a festive touch. Twinkle lights can be used as subtle accents indoors, in and among plants.

Balloons:

Helium balloon groupings are animated, they are an open invitation for guests to relax and enjoy the fun. Balloons are useful to highlight focal points such as buffet, beverage and wedding cake table, also serving stations and guest book registry. Balloon groupings can soften the tent's silhouette, direct guests to and from washroom facilities and parking area with color coded balloons. Select balloons in your wedding color theme or use a variety of colors. Tie each balloon with a long ribbon (6 feet) so that you can secure a group together with soft bows and silk flowers. Inflate the balloons yourself (or assign team members) by leasing the equipment or ask your florist or balloon specialist to attend to this.

Wedding Site Diagram:

An easy way to plan your home and out-of-door wedding is to create a simple scale drawing of the area to be used, indicting where key activities will take place. Include scale drawings of equipment and furniture that will be used in the ceremony and reception, these are called templates. It's a lot easier to move paper on paper than moving heavy equipment when you have a scale overview in front of you. Measure the wedding site, and with graph paper, use a ratio of 1 foot equals 1/2 inch. Use the same proportions for equipment and furniture when making templates (1 foot equals 1/2 inch). Make templates in contrasting colored paper of equipment (tables, chairs, tent, wedding arch, rose trellis, gazebo, serving stations, trees, plats, etc.) When you have decided what goes where, make up copies of the plan for those assisting you as they can direct the delivery of supplies and equipment. If you are unable to draft the scale map and templates, ask your schools to recommend one of their design students to take on the project for a small fee, or if you have hired the services of a landscape gardener, they can take this project on for you.

HOUSE OF WORSHIP:

Book an appointment soon to confirm the availability of cleric and house of worship on your wedding date. If you are not a member of the church, synagogue or mosque, you may not be given a firm commitment on your wedding date until a few months before the event. Their own members are given first priority. If you are planning to live in the community, this may be a good time to establish roots by joining this house of worship.

Detail everything in your contract; date and time of arrival and departure, fees and gratuities. Be very clear on regulations for the use of : sanctuary, cleric, organist and custodial services, choice of music and musicians, scripting your own vows, limitations on photography during the wedding ceremony, decoration set up, tear down and cleaning premises. Ask what equipment the house of worship will allow you to use: vases, stands, candle sticks, kneeling benches etc. If the house of worship contract states that your flowers must remain in the sanctuary after the ceremony, make arrangements to share flower expenses with a couple that may be also getting married there on the same day. Pre-marital counselling may be required for all brides and grooms before the wedding. Record the name and phone number of your contact person. Be sure to have every detail in writing .

Women's groups affiliated with the houses of worship have some wonderful cooks who are available to cater weddings. One of these women may even specialize in creating wedding cakes. Keep this in mind.

WEDDING CHAPEL:

Marrying couples have discovered that wedding chapels have less regulations than a house of worship and offer special packages in conjunction with their wedding service such as: photographic/ videography, transportation, special effects, decorations and accommodations. Some of these facilities are tiny and will not accommodate a large wedding. Ask what the capacity seating is in the chapel before making a firm commitment to avoid disappointment. Confirm in writing your date, time of arrival and departure, and specific services you require, and name and phone number of contact person.

WEDDING CEREMONY EQUIPMENT RENTAL:

Special equipment for your wedding ceremony, such as a tent, canopy, vase, stand, wedding arch, gazebo, rose trellis, kneeling bench and candle sticks, can be leased for the event. Refer to the yellow pages in your telephone directory for this service.

WEDDING VOWS:

A vow is a solemn promise that bonds two people with a very specific understanding. Thus, it is important for each person to find the words to express what they promise to give and what expectations they have in return, in marriage. Doing so expresses in their own voice, the commitment and purpose of this union. Marriage, when understood as a committed relationship, is an opportunity for enormous personal and spiritual growth for each individual. The following poem reflects on these thoughts.

Relationships

When it comes to relationships, I know this is true,
I can still be me and be loved by you.

We can accept each other with love and care,
Then find all the ways in which we can share.

A wonderful life with our focus on spirit,
If we would open our minds and our hearts just to hear it.

How much we would grow and find that rare place,
Where we could all have that love and still have our space.

It will take some work, communication and such,
I know that we're worth it, so let's stay in touch.

Sculpt in stone those rare moments, make them often, why not?
The prize we're both seeking is worth our best shot.

As you polish each facet of your rare gem, so true,
I'll be working on me...so I'll be worthy of you.

Don Petrucelle 1997

Resource material to consider when scripting your own vows are; sacred writings, (Bible, Torah, Koran) and favorite poems or verse. Visit your library. There is a vast selection of fine material suitable for your wedding vows. "I Do" by Sydney Barbara Metrick is a good source for planning your ceremony and has appropriate quotations. Richard Leviton's excellent book, "Weddings by Design" is a guide to non-traditional wedding ceremonies. Consult with your clergy or civil officiant for legality of scripting your own vows in your region.

My daughter Gaebrielle and her husband James consulted with their minister who customized their vows to reflect their promises. They have agreed to share their wedding vows with you.

Marriage Ceremony
Gaebrielle Lisette and James Gregory
December 21, 1996

This is a special day, winter solstice, this is the day when the sun turns and begins its journey back to its full brightness. From this day forward there will be ever increasing light in our journey, in our lives, in our hearts. This is a most auspicious day, a day of celebration. We have gathered here to bear witness to the joining of two beautiful people, Gaebrielle Lisette and James Gregory, in the state of holy matrimony.

Let us begin by closing our eyes and taking a deep breath. As we inhale the life force together, we invoke the presence of God and Goddess, the Essence of Mother Earth and Great Spirit. We ask this Spirit to flow through all creation, bless this ceremony, bless this gathering, this celebration of life. We ask that Great Spirit be with us always, guiding, protecting, supporting and inspiring each of us. We ask a special blessing for Gaebrielle and James, that their Union be strong, their home be filled with light and love. May they walk together in Peace. We ask that their hearts be filled with courage to face the challenges of life. And that they look first to God for strength and clarity, and then share that clarity and wisdom with each another. We ask the blessings of Mother Earth to be with them all their days, bringing bounty and good fortune to them always. For these blessings we give thanks. Amen.

Gaebrielle and James, today you are coming together to give birth to a new presence, your relationship with each another. This presence will take on a life of its own from this day forward. It must be nurtured as a new-born child. It will create a strength that is greater than the sum of its parts. To walk this path consciously, to work, and love and live as a team, it is important to make conscious the foundation upon which you will build. Some of the elements we have spoken about include: love... respect... truth... support... tenderness... admiration... understanding... sensitivity and loyalty.

My question is this, how will you know when you are loved? How will you know when you are supported? How will you know when you are understood? I ask you now to make a commitment to speak with each another, to ask for what you need and what you want, to communicate openly and often, to keep the flow. Are you ready and willing to do this? I ask you to promise each another that you will spend some time daily and weekly thinking and speaking about these things... I feel loved when you say this... I feel loved when you do that... I feel cherished when... I would like you to promise each another that you will ask for help in your relationship and in your lives when you need it. Are you ready to agree to disagree, to honor your differences, to allow them to bring a richness of experience to your lives? Are you willing to agree to let there be spaces in your togetherness, and let the winds of heaven dance between you? Are you ready to promise to love each another, and to love yourselves... and let your love be like the waves of the ocean, moving between the shores of your souls?

Do you, Gaebrielle Lisette, take this man, James Gregory, to be your lawful, wedded husband, to love, respect and cherish, each and every day of your lives together? " I do."

Do you, James Gregory, take this woman, Gaebrielle Lisette, to be your lawful wedded wife, to love, respect and cherish, each and every day of your life together? "I do."

Gaebrielle: "With this ring, I thee wed."

James: "With this ring, I thee wed."

May the song of your life be joyous, and let each one of you stand clearly in your own essence, as the strings of a harp are close to each another though they sing their own music. By the power invested in me, I pronounce you Husband and Wife. God Bless you; walk in Peace.

LEGAL REQUIREMENTS:

Book your clergy or civil officiant early to avoid disappointment. Record the name and phone number of contact person. Ask your clergy or civil officiant what is legally required in your region to be wed: marriage license, blood tests, medical, birth certificates and scripting your own vows.

CHECK LIST FOR HOME AND OUT-OF-DOOR WEDDING

Preparing the Home and Out-Of-Door Space:
Seasonal Cleaning
Carpets _____ Floors _____
Drapes _____ Curtains _____
Windows _____ Furniture _____
Cleaning Service _____ Phone _____

Repairs and maintenance
Carpenter _____ Phone _____
Electrician _____ Phone _____
Plumber _____ Phone _____
Painter _____ Phone _____
Handyman _____ Phone _____
Storage of following items _____
Storage Unit _____ Phone _____
Truck Rental _____ Phone _____

Garden Plan
Perennials _____
Bulbs _____
Annuals _____
Landscape Gardening Service _____ Phone _____
Tool Shed Items Stored _____
Parking Spaces _____ Valet Parking _____

Equipment Leasing
Canopy _____ Awning _____ Tent _____
Tables _____ Chairs _____ Benches _____

Fountain _____ Gazebo _____ Wedding Arch _____

Dance Floor _____Sound Equipment _____

Plants _____ Hanging Baskets _____

Equipment Leasing Company: _____

Address _____

Contact person _____ Phone _____

Total cost _____ Deposit _____ Payment schedule _____

Hosting Your Wedding At Leased Or Remote Facilities:

If you are leasing facilities from a commercial, municipal or private concern, your contract should detail everything you are buying. Yes, even when using facilities from friends or family, clearly enter in writing what you have agreed upon.

Confirm the availability of facilities on your wedding date_____

Time frame to use facilities, date for: Set up _____

Tear down _____ Clean up _____

      Interior Space

Capacity _____

Description of rooms for your use (dining, kitchen, toilet etc.) _____

_____

Furnishings included for use _____

Rules and regulations on premises _____

* For ceremony equipment refer to "Check List For Wedding Ceremony"

Equipment for food preparation, serving, cleaning for use _____

Grills _____Refrigeration _____

Food serving _____ Storage _____

Catering equipment needed (refer to Chapter 5) _____

_____

Supplies: Soap _____ Hand towels _____ Toilet tissue _____

      Exterior Space

Capacity _____

Description of area for your use: Perimeters _____

Fireplace _____Storage _____ Other _____

Tables _____ Seating, chairs _____

Covered shelter _____ Ornaments _____

Parking _____ Valet parking _____

Food preparation equipment: Grills _____ Refrigeration _____

Storage _____ Serving _____

Services: Landscaping _____

Water hook up _____ Electrical hook up _____

Electrical generator _____

Services provider:

Landscaper _____ Phone_____

Power Company _____ Phone _____

Water Company _____ Phone _____
Electrician _____ Phone _____
Plumber _____ Phone _____
Handyman _____ Phone _____
Name of leased facility _____
Address _____
Contact person _____ Phone _____
Facility cost _____ Deposit _____ Payment schedule _____
Cancellation policy _____

Decorating The Wedding:

Detail all of the equipment that you have leased and reconfirm that it will be available on your
wedding date_____ Time of delivery _____ Time of pick up _____
Tent _____ Canopy _____Awning _____
Gazebo _____ Wedding Arch _____
Rose trellis _____ Fountain _____
Hanging potted flowers _____ Plants _____
Citronella candles _____ Stage _____
Dance floor _____ Sound Equipment _____
Twinkle lights _____ Lantern _____
Balloons _____ Inflating equipment _____
Sew-it-yourself wedding decorations (refer to Chapter 6) _____
Wedding site diagram _____
Equipment leasing company _____
Address _____
Contact person _____ Phone _____
Cost _____ Deposit _____ Payment schedule _____
Cancellation policy _____

Wedding Ceremony Equipment:

Detail all of the equipment you have leased and reconfirm that it will be available on your
wedding date _____ Time of delivery _____ Time of pick up _____
Kneeling bench _____Wedding arches _____
Canopy _____ Tent _____
Vase _____ Candelabra _____Candlesticks _____
Gazebo _____ Rose trellis _____
Name of leasing company _____
Address _____
Contact person _____ Phone _____
Cost _____ Deposit _____Payment schedule _____
Cancellation policy _____

House of Worship and Wedding Chapel Ceremony:
Confirm availability on your wedding date :
House of Worship _____Capacity _____
Wedding chapel _____ Capacity _____
Fees and gratuities for:
Clergy _____
Organist _____
Musician _____
Custodian _____
Rules and restrictions for use of facilities:
House of Worship _____
Wedding Chapel _____
Pre-marital counselling requirements _____
Music selections   _____
Musicians _____
Vows:
Traditional _____
Original _____
Restrictions on photography and videography during wedding ceremony _____
_____
Time limitations for:
Decoration set up _____ Tear down _____ Cleaning _____
Other wedding services are offered _____
Must flowers remain in the sanctuary after the ceremony? _____ If so
what cost sharing arrangements can be made with other weddings being performed the same
day _____
Equipment available to use for the wedding _____
Wedding rings _____ Caretaker of rings _____
Name of House of Worship or Wedding Chapel _____
Address _____
Contact person _____ phone _____
Cost _____ Deposit _____ Payment schedule _____
Cancellation policy _____
     Wedding Ceremony Equipment
Detail all equipment leased and cost per item. Confirm its availability on your wedding date
Delivery date/time _____ Pick up date/time _____
Canopy _____ Tent _____
Candelabra _____ Candlesticks _____
Wedding arch _____ Gazebo _____ Rose trellis _____
Kneeling bench _____ Vase _____
Rental Equipment Company _____
Address _____
Contact person _____ Phone _____

Cost _____ Deposit _____ Payment schedule _____

Cancellation policy _____

Legal Requirements

Marriage licence _____ Blood tests _____ Birth certificates _____

Medical _____ Other _____

Will cleric/civil officiant travel to your wedding ceremony site ?_____

fees _____ travel expense _____

Legal restrictions in your state for scripting your own vows_____

Contact person _____ Phone _____

Wedding Vows

Sacred:

source _____

_____

_____

Secular:

source_____

_____

_____

Chapter 5

WEDDING RECEPTION

SELF-CATERED RECEPTION

Menu Selection and Catering:

A self-catered wedding reception is a realistic choice when carefully planned ahead. There are several ways to approach this. Since many recipes can be cooked in advance and frozen until needed, you can prepare the food yourself a week or so before the wedding. If family and friends want to help by preparing a dish, supply them with the ingredients to prepare it at their homes and bring to the reception. Another approach is to select from the menu offered by restaurants, delicatessens or supermarkets. They will prepare the food for your reception and if they don't deliver, you can arrange to have it picked up.

After you have created a wedding menu, purchase all the ingredients and prepare an intimate candlelight dinner for two. This will enable you to estimate the cost per person for your wedding reception and give you both an opportunity to change the menu around to suit your event and budget. Enter the final cost in your budget check list. Just before the wedding, supply each "team" cook with ingredients for the dish they will prepare. If all the food is being prepared in your kitchen let volunteers or hired staff know where supplies are stored. Clarify with "team" members what tasks need to be done and when it needs to be done. If you do not have all the food preparation, warming, cooling and serving equipment, borrow what you need from friends and family or lease from an equipment rental company.

Organizing the space for your reception depends upon the number of guests invited and the amount of space with which you have to work. If you plan a sit down affair you have two options; serve from one large table situated indoors or in a climate controlled tent on the lawn or arrange several small tables and chairs indoors on the verandah or inside a tent on the lawn. Instructions for decorating tables and chairs are found in Chapter 6. A buffet style event requires less space, accommodates a greater number of guests and enables you to do a lot of the preparation in advance. Food, dinnerware, cutlery and beverage can all be placed on one table as illustrated in Chapter 7, or divided into two or three smaller serving stations and placed indoors or out-of-doors. When space permits arrange small tables and chairs in intimate groupings for seating of guests. Although, if you want to place a time limit on your reception (one to two hours), decrease the number of chairs so that guests are not encouraged to linger beyond the designated time.

Wedding Cake:

The flavor and style of your wedding cake is a personal choice: chocolate, hazelnut or amaretto with cream, fruit or liquor filling, garnished with fresh flowers or glazed fruit. There are five cake, tort and flan recipes in Chapter 7 that are suitable for your wedding cake. Home-bake specialists or perhaps a talented friend will bake and decorate your wedding cake. Home-bake specialists supply many fine restaurants and catering companies with their gourmet creations. Ask friends, bakeries or restaurants to recommend names of wedding cake bakers or consider having a local bakery or supermarket perform this service. Discuss the style, flavor and decoration of your cake with the baker of choice, and of course, sample their cake. Display wedding cake table out of the flow of traffic where it can be seen but not damaged. Decorate the table top with flowers or bowls of fruit and nuts. Have a cake knife, dessert plates and forks at the wedding cake table, refer to Chapter 7. Arrange for a "team" member to continue cutting and serving wedding cake after you have posed for photographers. Instructions for making tablecloths for the wedding cake table is found in Chapter 6.

Catering Equipment Rental:

All the equipment required to host a successful wedding reception can be leased from an equipment rental company: attractive climate controlled tents, furnishings, dance floor, sound system, portable commode and equipment necessary for food preparation, warming, cooling and serving. An electrical generator can be leased to provide all the amenities of an urban environment in a remote setting; lighting, heating, entertainment, whatever your heart desires. Refer to the yellow pages for listing of equipment leasing companies. Ask for and research references and better business ratings. Confirm the availability of all equipment you need and ensure it is in good running order. Inquire about delivery and pick up service to your location. Detail all of this in writing. Inspect all shipments upon delivery to be sure it matches what you have ordered. Keep in mind that some wine stores have a stemware loan-with-wine-purchase service and will deliver this with your wine or champagne order.

Staff:

Discuss in advance with volunteer "team" members or hired staff what help is needed: furniture and equipment set up, cooking, food and beverage serving, landscaping, valet parking, washing and cleaning up. Draw up a schedule, listing names and phone numbers of "team" volunteers or staff and where necessary supplies and equipment are stored. If your wedding is to be held in a remote locale, list the names and phone numbers of a reliable electrician, plumber, carpenter and handyman.

PROFESSIONAL CATERING SERVICE:

Catering:

Good caterers are reserved months in advance so start planning and interview early. If you have a special menu in mind (vegetarian, kosher, diabetic), look for a caterer that will work with you on this. There are several catering service options available to you; private catering or full service and limited service commercial catering. A private catering service, usually a one person business, will prepare the entire menu in your kitchen and may or may not arrange to have all the necessary equipment and serving staff for your event. Full service commercial caterers will attend to every detail: food preparation, delivery, equipment rental, set up, clean up, food serving, bartending, liquor and liquor license, beverages, wedding cake cutting and serving. Limited service caterers will supply the bare essentials of preparing and delivering the food from your menu. When interviewing a catering service, detail all the staff and serving equipment required so you can make necessary arrangements. Before signing a contract, taste their food and detail all services provided by the caterer. Ask what deposit, fees and gratuities are expected. Ask for and research the caterers references and better business rating.

Wedding cake:

Some private and commercial catering companies will supply your wedding cake; if not ask them to recommend a local bakery or a home-bake-specialist. Discuss the style and flavor you want for your wedding cake and cake decorating. Commercial caterers will charge from $1.50 to $3.00 per guest to cut and serve your wedding cake. To cut costs, assign a "team" member to cut and serve the cake after the bride and groom have performed the cake cutting ritual for guests and the photographer.

Staff:

Clarify with your caterer the extent of services they will provide. If additional serving staff is needed, ask friends and family for recommendations or advertise for students who've had restaurant experience. Assign a "team" member to work with the caterer so that you will be free to enjoy your wedding guests. If you are planning a small reception ask for volunteer "team" members to set out and replenish food and beverage.

CHECK LIST FOR WEDDING RECEPTION
Self Catered Reception:
Menu selection

Hors d' oeuvres _____

Brunch _____

Luncheon _____

Afternoon Tea _____

Buffet _____

Twilight Dessert _____

Wedding cake _____

White wine _____ Red wine _____

Champagne _____ Punch _____

Liquor _____ Liquor permit _____

Tea _____ Coffee _____

Cost per person from menu _____

Food Preparation:

Recipe and ingredients   Prepared by   Delivery: date/time

_____

_____

_____

_____

_____

_____

_____

_____

_____

_____

_____

Wedding Cake:

Style and flavor _____

Decoration _____

Baker _____

Set up and display _____

Catering Equipment Rental:

Confirm that all catering equipment is available on your wedding date _____

Tablecloths _____ Napkins _____

Dinnerware_____

Cutlery _____ Glassware _____ Stemware _____

Coffee maker _____ Tea pots _____

Chafing dishes_____ Warming tables _____

Food serving equipment _____ Utensils _____Trays _____

Ice chest _____ Spring water dispenser _____

Leasing company name. _____

Address _____

Contact person _____ Phone _____

Total cost _____ deposit _____ payment schedule_____

cancellation policy _____

Staff, Setting Up For Reception:

Task   "Team" or staff   Date/time

_____

_____

_____

_____

_____

_____

_____

_____

_____

Professional catering:
Private catering, Full service catering and Limited service catering

Confirm caterers availability on wedding date _____ Cost per person from menu _____

Hors d'oeuvres _____

Main course _____

Dessert _____

Coffee _____ Tea _____

Red wine _____ White wine _____

Champagne _____ Liquor _____

Corkage fee _____ Liquor permit _____

Fees and gratuities:

Food preparation _____ Serving _____

Wedding cake: Baking _____ Decoration _____

Cutting and serving per guest _____

Catering service name _____

Address _____

Contact person _____ Phone _____

Total cost _____ Deposit _____ Payment schedule _____

Cancellation policy _____

Staff:

If using a private catering or limited service catering service refer to "Self-Catered Check List For Staff."

Catering Equipment:

If using a private catering or limited service catering service refer to "Self-Catered Check List For Catering Equipment Rental."

Chapter 6

DECORATE WITH SEW-IT-YOURSELF WEDDING ACCESSORIES

WEDDING ACCESSORIES

Create unique custom table treatments for your wedding in a color scheme that you plan for your home. In doing so, you can use them again for future social occasions. With careful planning, all of your creative energies now can be put to good use in the years to come, not to mention a gift to yourself of lovely household linens. In this chapter sew-it-yourself instructions are given for tablecloth variations, placemats, chair cushions, napkins and napkin folding. If you have not already purchased a patio table and chairs, borrow or lease these for your out-of-door wedding celebration. Card table sets work indoors and out-of-doors to create intimate social spaces. Sew table cloth sets in coordinating solids, patterns and prints. Enlist the help of friends and family to create these lovely table decorations for your wedding or hire a seamstress.

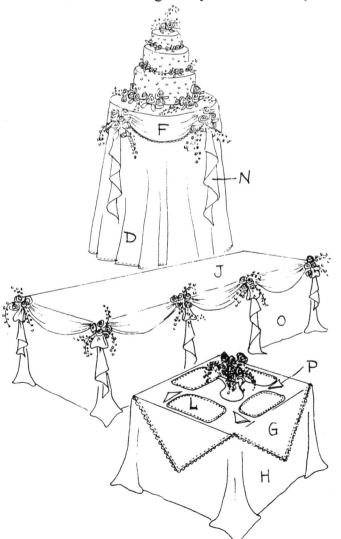

Swag tablecloth: round(F) rectangle or square (J) with jabots (N)
The "mock" swag tablecloth with jabots is a quick and easy project that creates a formal appearance for the head table, buffet table or wedding cake table. Combine satin, taffeta, voile or lace in same or complimentary colors (refer to chart at the end of this chapter for fabric suggestions).

Tablecloth variations: round ruffled (B) plain round (D) square (G, H) and rectangle (O)
Easy care, coordinated cotton fabrics are available in most fabric stores. Team a bold

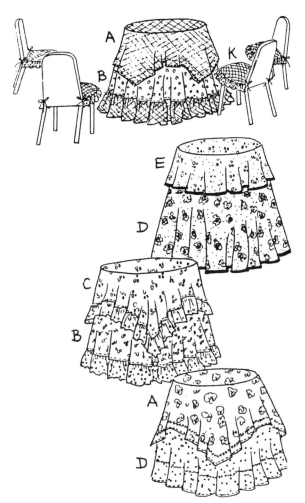

print with a demure print; a plaid with a light check in the same color family, a positive print against its negative counterpart, a pretty chintz or calico against a miniature in a coordinating color. Most sales assistants in fabric stores are very knowledgeable and will, no doubt, enjoy helping you with your project. Fabric stores are also an excellent source for locating a seamstress, should you need one.

Ruffled chair cushions (K)

Aside from the comfort, a chair cushion can transform an ordinary chair into a decorator piece. All that is required is fabric, thread and foam cushion to sew a ruffled chair cushion.

Placemats with variations (L)

Because these placemats are reversible they give double duty service and an added touch to the well dressed table. Used over the table cloth will soften the table surface and save the cloth from soiling.

Napkin lined or unlined (P)

Your well dressed table is now complete with matching napkins in tea or dinner size. You can sew these napkins single fabric thickness or double thickness (lined or unlined). The napkins are designed to coordinate with all of your table decorations.

Fancy folded napkins

Experiment with plain and fancy folded napkins and a downright practical "Jelly roll" folded napkin containing the cutlery. Easy step-by step illustrated instructions will enable your "team" members to assist you in this task. See page 65 for these instructions.

MAKING A PAPER PATTERN FOR A ROUND TABLE CLOTH

Begin by measuring the table diameter plus twice the desired drop of the tablecloth plus one inch for the hem. This is the total size of your tablecloth. Divide this figure by two, and use it to make your pattern. Fold a large sheet of *paper into quarters. Hold the end of a yardstick at the inside corner of the folded paper and with a pencil draw a quarter circle (like a compass) at the desired size you want for your tablecloth. Cut along the pencil line (through all 4 thickness) and open. You now have a paper pattern for your tablecloth.

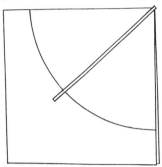

*Purchase roll paper at a paper store or party shop, or tape newspaper together until you have the size needed.

MEASURING, LAYOUT, CUTTING AND SEWING INSTRUCTIONS

Swag tablecloth: round (F)

Measure the diameter of the table plus twice the desired drop of the cloth plus one inch for the hem. If the tablecloth you plan to make is 60" round or square, then your pattern will fit perfectly on 60" wide fabric. If your paper pattern extends beyond the width of the fabric (for example if the fabric is 45" wide) then you will need to join the fabric for your tablecloth. Make two seams on each side of the center section. Avoid a center seam.

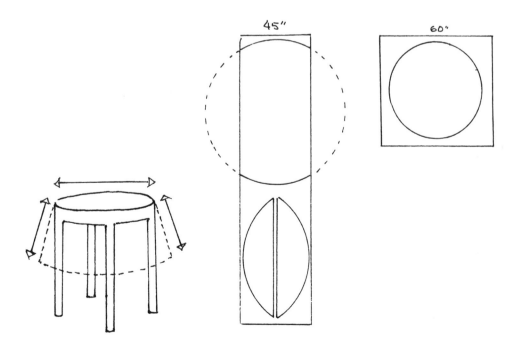

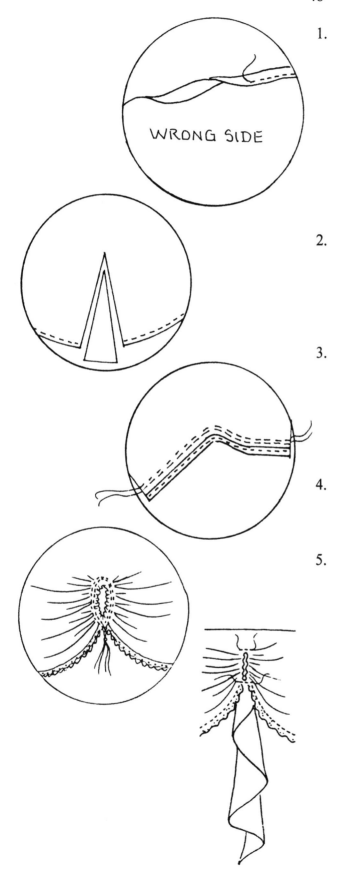

WRONG SIDE

1. Place center of pattern on the fabric, fold pattern that extends beyond the fabric to the center, cut each piece off and redraw the three pattern pieces, increasing the width on cut edges by 1/2" (seams where it will be joined). This ensures the correct width of the finished tablecloth. After you have created a paper pattern, lay the pattern on fabric, cut and stitch together.

2. Press a narrow 1/4" hem, fold over again 1/4", press and stitch. * If making up a tablecloth of lace, stitch 1/2" lace trim to right side over raw edge.

3. For "mock" swags, divide tablecloth into quarters, create a "pie shape" by marking each quarter with pins 10-1/2" deep by 2-1/2" wide. Cut away the "pie." Press a narrow hem and stitch.

4. Machine baste (6 stitches to the inch) a double row the full length of the "pie" leaving pull threads at both ends.

5.   Tie four baste threads together at one end of the "pie." Collect two baste threads from TOP and gently pull to desired gathers for your swag, tie a knot and clip excess thread. Arrange gathers to form an attractive swag effect.

Position jabot behind the swag and stitch into place.

* Select (B) or (D) lower round table cloth to compliment your swag table cloth. Refer to page 51 for instructions for these tablecloths.

Swag tablecloth, rectangle (J)

Measure the width of the table top plus twice the desired drop of your tablecloth by the length of the table top plus twice the desired drop of the tablecloth. Remember to add 1" hem allowance. If the width of your rectangle or square table exceeds the width of your fabric then a join is necessary. Place the seam of this join in the tablecloth lengthwise.

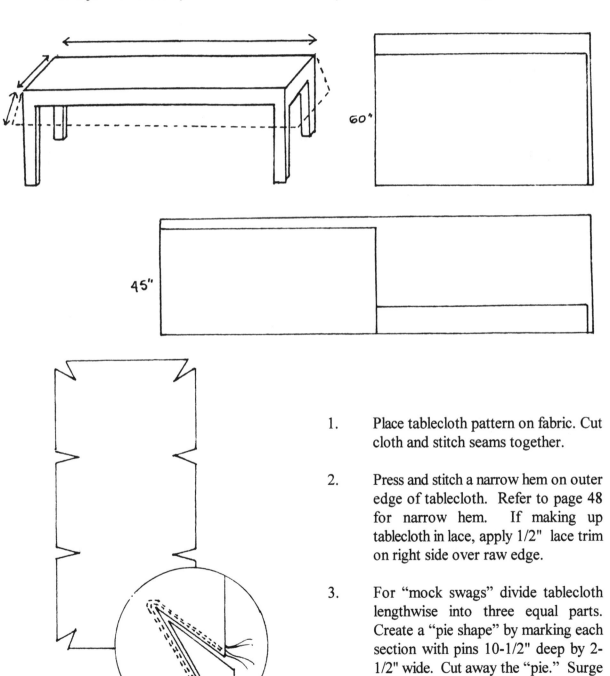

1. Place tablecloth pattern on fabric. Cut cloth and stitch seams together.

2. Press and stitch a narrow hem on outer edge of tablecloth. Refer to page 48 for narrow hem. If making up tablecloth in lace, apply 1/2" lace trim on right side over raw edge.

3. For "mock swags" divide tablecloth lengthwise into three equal parts. Create a "pie shape" by marking each section with pins 10-1/2" deep by 2-1/2" wide. Cut away the "pie." Surge or press and stitch a narrow hem.

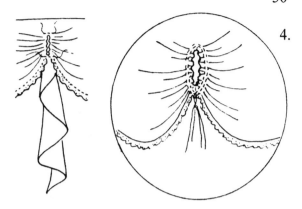

4. Refer to steps 4 and 5 on page 48 to complete the "mock swag" tablecloth.

Position jabot behind the swag and stitch into place.

* Select lower rectangle (O) on page 56, to compliment your swag tablecloth.

Fabric combination suggestions:

Listed are some fabric combination suggestions for the swag tablecloth, lower tablecloth and the jabot. Use your imagination while visiting a fabric store see what 'feels' right for your event. Some sales assistants in fabric stores are quite well-informed and will be able to show you some of their specialty fabrics in stock.

Lower Tablecloth FABRIC	COLOR	Swag Tablecloth FABRIC	COLOR	Jabots FABRIC	COLOR
Moire	pastel	Taffeta	white	Taffeta	white
Taffeta	white	Taffeta	pastel	Taffeta	white
"	pastel	Lace	white	Taffeta	white
"	white	Nylon tule	white	Taffeta	white
"	white	Voile	white	Taffeta	white
"	pastel	Embroidered Eyelet	white	Taffeta	white
Embroidered Eyelet	white	Embroidered Eyelet	pastel	Satin	white
"	pastel		white	Satin	white
"	white	Voile	white	Satin	white
Polished Cotton	muted print	Polished cotton Moire	white	Satin	white
"	moire white	"	Pastel	Satin	white
Cotton	pastel	Cotton	white	Cotton	white
Cotton	muted print	Cotton	pastel	Cotton	pastel
Cotton	white	Organdy	white	Satin	white
Cotton	white	Nylon net	white	Taffeta	white

51

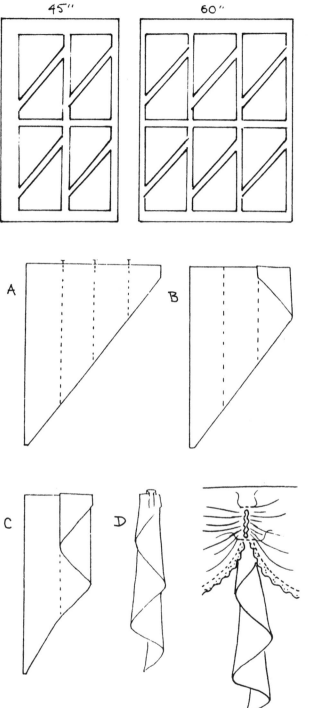

Jabots (N)

Measure the desired length of the jabot by 17" wide. Select fabric that drapes easily by referring to chart on page 50.

1. Cut a paper pattern following diagram using the pattern layout guide. Calculate the amount of fabric required by measuring the length of the jabot, by 17" wide plus the number you need and whether they are lined or unlined. For lined jabots double the fabric requirement. If your jabots are unlined, finish with a rolled hem.

2. Place the pattern on the fabric, pin in place and cut the jabots.

Single thickness: Apply a narrow hem (page 48) along the sides, top and diagonal edge.

Lined jabots: sew right sides together leaving a 3" opening at the top. Turn right side out, press and stitch opening.

(A) Divide jabot into four equal parts (4-1/4"), vertically, mark with pins.

(B) Fold first quarter over toward the front to the marker, pin in place.

(C) Fold second quarter toward the back to the marker, pin in place.

(D) Fold the last quarter over, stitch in place. Form an inverted pleat at the top. Jabot width at the top will measure 2-1/2." Place each jabot inside the swag tablecloth at the gathered point; stitch into place.

Plain round tablecloth, upper (E) lower (D)

Refer to instructions for table measuring, paper pattern making and fabric layout for round tablecloth on page 46. For a lined tablecloth you will need twice the amount of fabric (same or contrast fabric). Apply one of three hem finishes: narrow hem, rick-rack, bias binding.

Narrow hem: press 1/4," fold 1/4" press and stitch.

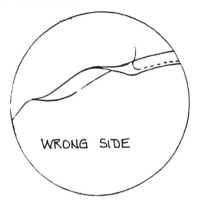

Bias binding hem: Open bias binding, lay flat on tablecloth edge with right sides together. Pin and stitch..

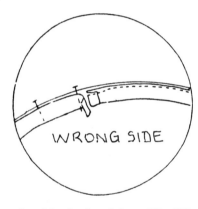

Apply **rick-rack** after a narrow hem has been stitched in place.

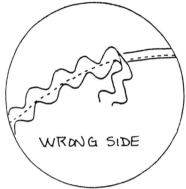

Fold bias over to opposite side, press and stitch close to the edge.

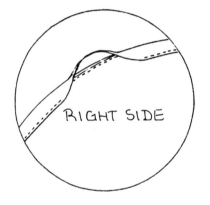

Round tablecloth with ruffle (B):
Refer to instruction for table measuring, making a paper pattern and fabric layout for round tablecloth on page 46. To calculate additional amount of fabric required for ruffle, multiply the diameter of tablecloth by 3.25, then multiply by 2. Cut a paper pattern for ruffle, 7-1/2" wide by the length required for a folded ruffle.

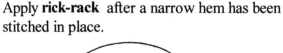

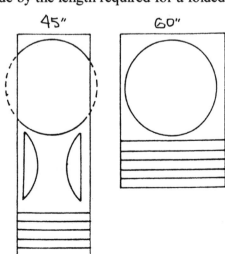

1. Measure and layout tablecloth. Cut and stitch seams together.

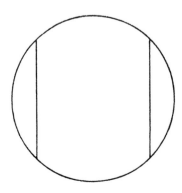

2. Join ruffle strips end to end and stitch until it forms a circle. Press seams flat. Fold lengthwise and press.

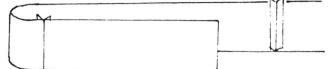

3. Divide ruffle circle into quarters and mark with pins.. Stitch double rows of a basting stitch (6 stitches to the inch) between markers leaving adequate pull threads to form gathers.

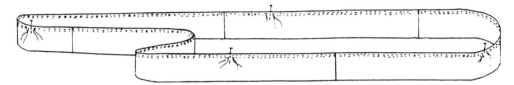

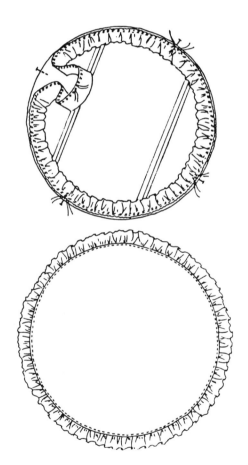

4. Divide tablecloth into quarters on(right side of fabric) and mark with pins. Match quarter markers on tablecloth with quarter sections on ruffle, pin into place on the right side of tablecloth. Collect top baste threads, pull gently until gathers are uniform, pin into place and stitch. Surge or use a zig zag stitch on the edge where the ruffle meets the tablecloth to prevent fraying. Top stitch where ruffle meets the tablecloth.

Lined tablecloth: If you want your tablecloth to give you double service, then line it. Cut another "same size" round tablecloth in the same fabric or in a contrast color or print, place over tablecloth after the ruffle has been attached, right sides together (like a sandwich). Pin in place and stitch along the edge leaving a 3" opening. Turn the tablecloth right side out, press and top stitch where the ruffle meets the tablecloth.

5. Press ruffles outward on the tablecloth and top stitch close to the edge.

Square tablecloth; plain (G) (H) (A) ruffled (C)
Measure the width of the table top plus twice the desired length of your tablecloth by the length of the table top plus twice the desired length of the tablecloth. Remember to add 1/2" hem allowance. If the width of your rectangle or square table exceeds the width of your fabric then a join is necessary. Place the seam- join lengthwise.

1. Layout instructions for square tablecloth on fabric 45" or 60" wide.

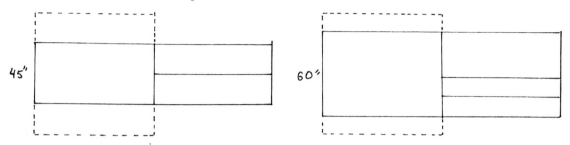

2. Apply one of three hem finishes: (A) narrow hem, (B) rick rack or (C) bias binding hem.

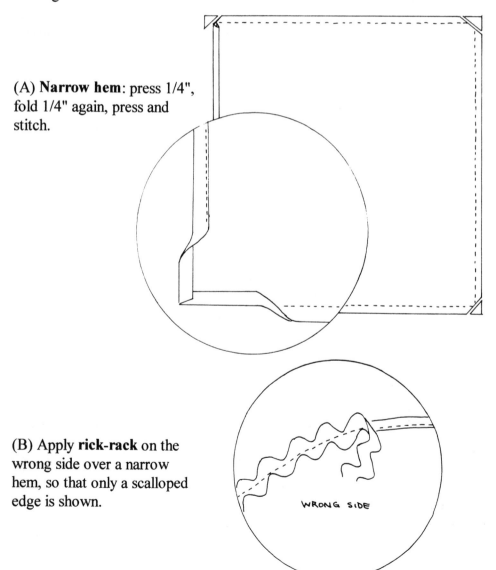

(A) **Narrow hem**: press 1/4", fold 1/4" again, press and stitch.

(B) Apply **rick-rack** on the wrong side over a narrow hem, so that only a scalloped edge is shown.

WRONG SIDE

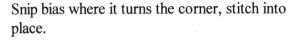

(C) **Bias binding hem**: Open bias binding "reinforce stitch" where bias will meet the corner before placing bias on to the cloth. Pin into place.

Snip bias where it turns the corner, stitch into place.

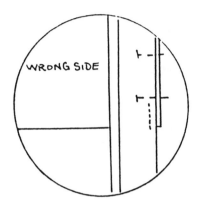

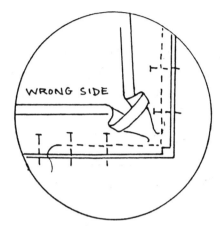

Bring inner edge of bias together, press to form mitred edge, stitch on pressing line. Clip excess mitred edge and corner.

Turn bias to wrong side, press and top stitch along seam and close to outer edge.

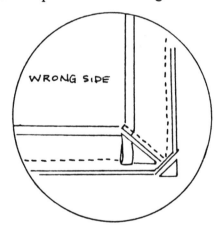

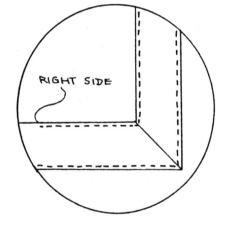

Square tablecloth with ruffle: (C)
Measure the width of the table top plus twice the desired length of your tablecloth by the length of the table top plus twice the desired length of the tablecloth. Remember to add 1/2" hem allowance. If the width of your tablecloth exceeds the width of your fabric, then a join is necessary. Calculate the amount of ruffle needed by measuring the total perimeter and multiply by 2. Layout square tablecloth with ruffle as directions indicate. Make a long paper pattern for the ruffle 7-1/2" wide . This folded ruffle will measure 3-1/4" wide when finished.

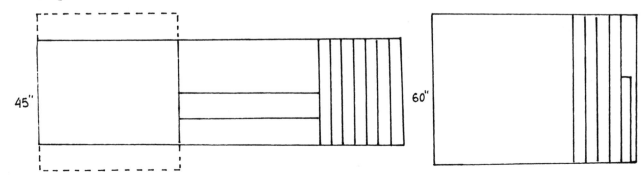

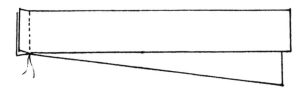

Join ruffle strips together lengthwise, until it forms a continuous circle; press seams flat.

Fold ruffle in half lengthwise and press. Divide into quarters, mark with pins. Stitch a double row of baste stitches, ending at each quarter leaving pull strings for gathering. Apply the ruffle and finish as per directions for round ruffled tablecloth on page 52.

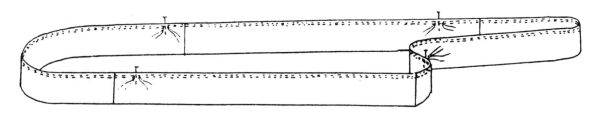

Rectangle tablecloth (O)

If a lower rectangular tablecloth is used underneath a swag tablecloth, measure the width of the table top plus twice the desired tablecloth drop by the length of the table top plus twice the desired tablecloth drop. Remember to add 1/2" hem allowance. If the width of your rectangle table exceeds the width of your fabric, then a join is necessary. Place the seam of this join in the tablecloth lengthwise.

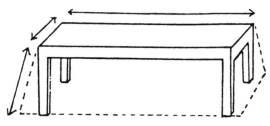

Layout and cut fabric 45" wide and 60" wide as shown.

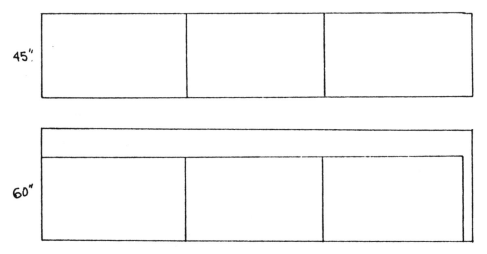

1. Join the three tablecloth sections on the lengthwise seams, surge or stitch.

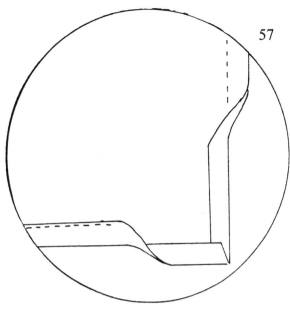

57

2. Finish with a **narrow hem**: stitch 1/4" around the edges, fold 1/4" and press. Fold 1/4" again, press and stitch.

Chair Cushions (K)

Purchase foam chair cushions close to the shape and size of your chairs. Measure length plus 2-1/2" (for ease and seams) and width plus 2-1/2" of purchased foam chair cushion.

Ruffle: measure the parameter of the cushion times two. Cut ruffle strips 7 -1/2" for a finished folded ruffle 3-1/4" wide. Fabric for ruffle can contrast or be the same as the cushion. By using a coordinating fabric on the ruffle and the bottom and top of the cushion, you will have greater decorating variety when used in your home later. The layout for chair cushions is merely a guide for your convenience and will vary according to the size of your chair and cushion.

Cushion ties: Measure and cut four 12" x 2-1/2" strips for each chair.

1. Join ruffle strips end to end and stitch until it forms one long strip. Press seams flat. Fold ruffle strip, wrong sides together, and press.

2. Divide ruffle strip into quarter sections and mark with pins. Baste two rows (6 stitches to the inch) on the outer edge, between markers. Leave enough length in the threads to pull gathers.

3. Pin ruffle quarters to the corners of the right side of the top chair cushion. Gently tug at "pull threads"until there is no slack, arrange gathers evenly. Stitch into place.

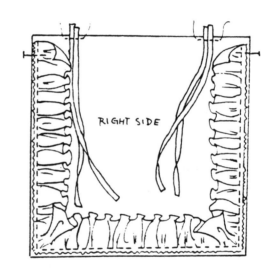

4. Chair ties: Fold over, one end of the chair tie 1/2" (widthwise, to give it a finished end). Fold each chair tie in half, lengthwise, press. Open flat and fold each lengthwise side 1/2" toward the center and press.

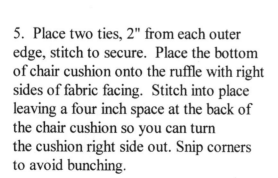

5. Place two ties, 2" from each outer edge, stitch to secure. Place the bottom of chair cushion onto the ruffle with right sides of fabric facing. Stitch into place leaving a four inch space at the back of the chair cushion so you can turn the cushion right side out. Snip corners to avoid bunching.

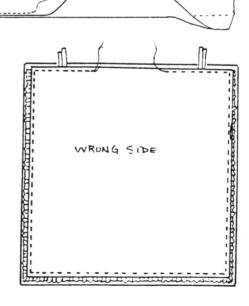

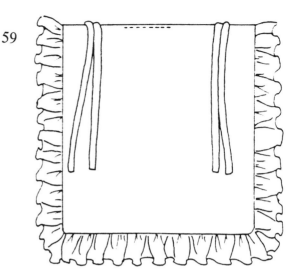

6. Pull cushion cover right side out, gently shaping around corners. Insert foam cushion. Baste stitch opening for easy removal of cover for laundering.

Placemats (L)

Instructions are given for oval and rectangle placemats that are lined, with three hem finishes: (A) Ruffled finish (B) Bias binding (3) Plain finish. Standard placemats measure 18" x 13."

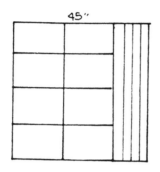

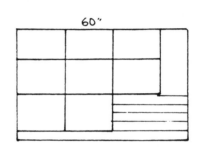

(A) Ruffled finish:

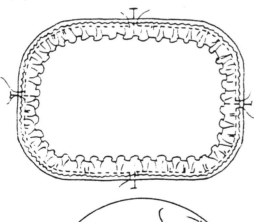

Oval placemat: refer to tablecloth for cutting, joining and gathering ruffle. Pin ruffle to oval placemat, easing around while gathering the ruffle. Stitch into place.

Rectangle placemat: bring ruffle to the corner, pin into place, continue around the corner pin into place. Stitch and proceed as follows:

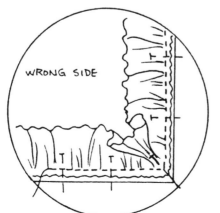

WRONG SIDE

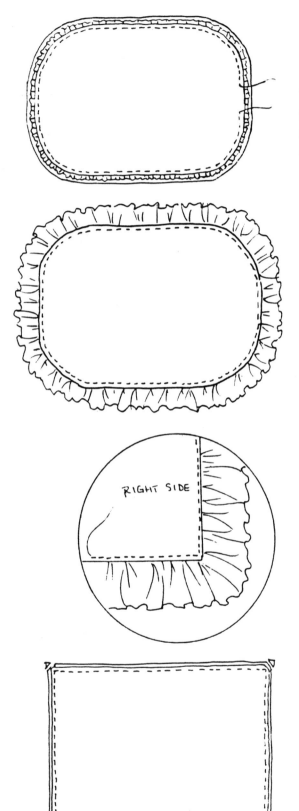

With right sides facing, place bottom of place mat over the top of ruffle, pin into place, stitch all around leaving a two-inch opening. Trim excess fabric to prevent bunching.

Turn placemat right-side-out, gently shaping. Press. Top stitch close to the edge.

(B) **Bias Binding for rectangle placemat.** With wrong sides facing, place top and bottom placemat together, pin and stitch. With purchased "double fold bias binding" open and place onto placemat, outer edges together and right sides together, pin into place and stitch.

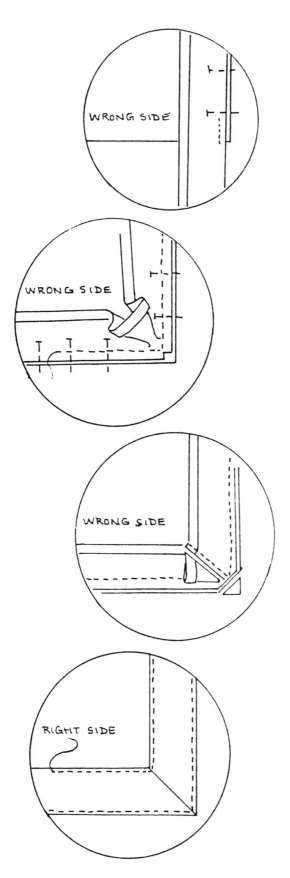

With purchased "double fold bias binding" open and place onto placemat, raw edges together, pin into place.

Before placing bias binding at corners, reinforce stitch the bias at that point, then continue by placing bias on the corner, pin in place, cut a notch to turn the corner smoothly, stitch.

Miter or bring together bias binding ends at each corner to form an angle, press down, stitch on the press mark.

Snip off mitered end and corner.

Turn bias binding over to opposite side, press. Stitch close to the edge where bias meets the placemat and on the outer edge for an attractive finish.

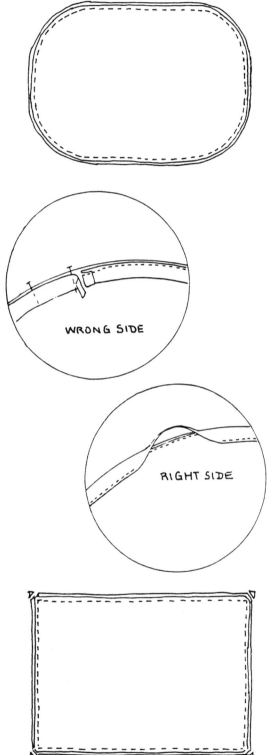

Bias Binding for oval placemat: with wrong sides together, place top and bottom placemat pin into place, stitch.

With purchased cotton "extra wide double fold bias binding", open and place on to placemat right sides and raw edges together, pin along outer edge of the placemat. Cut excess, fold end of bias over and stitch.

Turn bias binding over to opposite side, ease binding around the oval placemat, pin and stitch.

(C) **Plain finish; oval or square placemat:** With right sides together, place top and bottom placemat together, pin and stitch leaving a two inch opening.

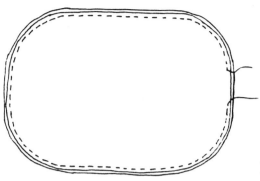

Trim excess seams and snip corners. Turn right side out, ease gently into shape and press.

Finish the plain placemat by applying top stitching close to the edge.

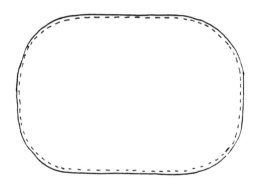

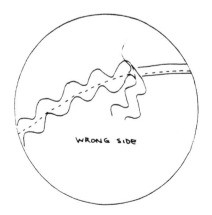

WRONG SIDE

If desired, add **rick rack** trim to finish this hem before top stitching is applied.

Napkins: (P) single thickness or lined napkins

Dinner napkin are 18" square; Tea Napkins are 9" square. Napkins can be single thickness, finished with a narrow hem or double thickness using same or contrast fabric. Layout and cutting directions are illustrated in solid and broken lines for single thickness and lined napkins. For 18" square dinner napkins you will need 1-1/8 yard single thickness and 2-1/4 yards double thickness on 45" wide fabric. With 60" wide fabric you will need 1-1/8 yard single thickness or 1-3/4 yard double thickness. Allow 1/2" for hem around the napkin. For 9" square tea napkins, use half the amount of fabric given for dinner napkins.

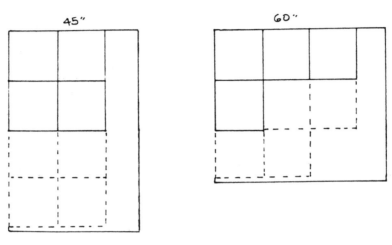

1. **Single thickness napkin**:
Finish with a narrow hem by applying a 1/4" baste stitch around napkin, snip off corners.

Fold at stitch line and press.

Fold 1/4" again, press and stitch.

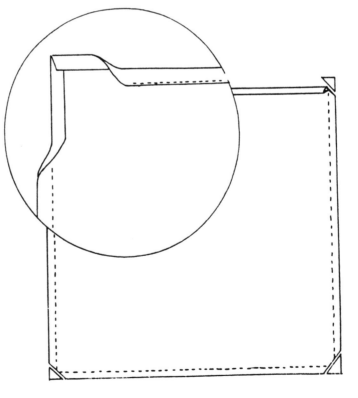

2. **Lined napkins:** With right sides together place top on to bottom napkin, pin into place. Stitch, leaving 1-1/2" opening. Snip corners.

Turn right side out, gently smoothing seams and corners, press.

To finish napkins apply a top stitch close to the edge all around napkin.

NAPKIN FOLDING

Your custom napkins will give your table an added distinction by using one of four napkin folds: Savoy, Lady Slipper, Tuxedo and Jelly Roll

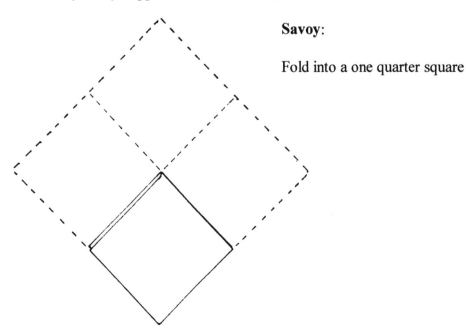

Savoy:

Fold into a one quarter square

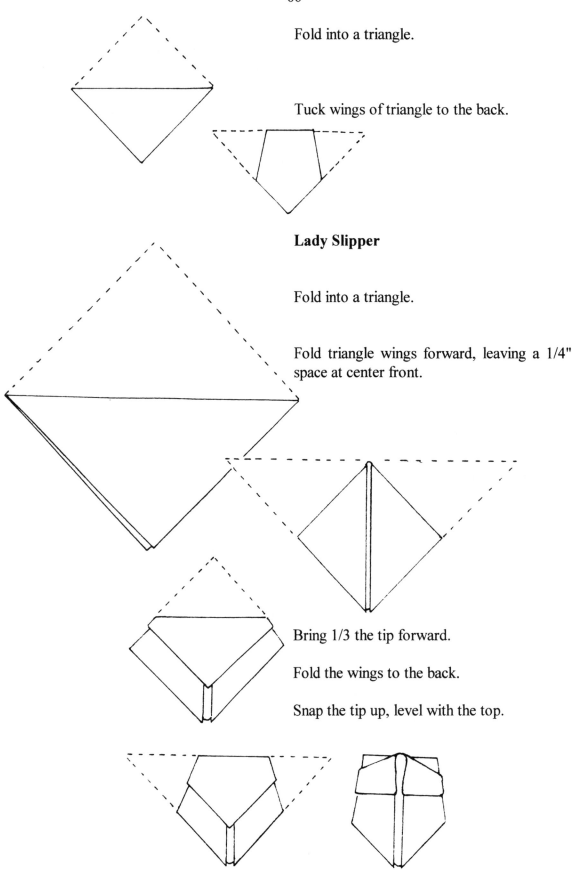

Fold into a triangle.

Tuck wings of triangle to the back.

Lady Slipper

Fold into a triangle.

Fold triangle wings forward, leaving a 1/4" space at center front.

Bring 1/3 the tip forward.

Fold the wings to the back.

Snap the tip up, level with the top.

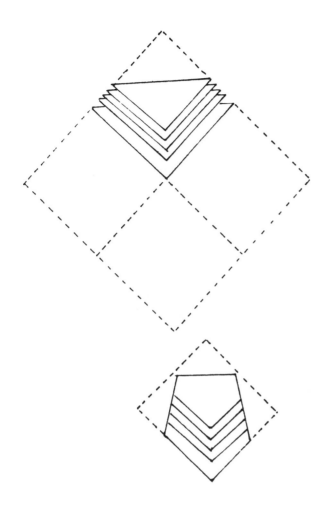

Tuxedo

Fold napkin into a one quarter square.

Fold first quarter point down to 1/4" of the opposite point. Fold the second quarter down to 1/4" of the opposite point. Repeat for third and fourth quarters.

Fold the top back.

Fold the 'wings to the back.

The Tuxedo fold looks smart with a lined napkin in a contrast color or print.

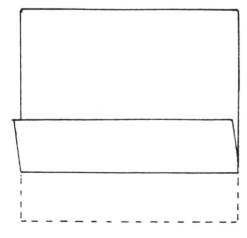

Jelly Roll

Bring bottom edge of square up to the half way mark.

Bring up the bottom edge up again to about the quarter mark. This will eventually be a pouch for the cutlery.

Turn over with fold facing down. Fold over lengthwise, leaving a 1-1/2" flap; fold this flap over.

Fold in half lengthwise to create a pouch for your cutlery. Insert cutlery and tie a bow with ribbon.

CHECK LIST FOR SEW-IT-YOURSELF WEDDING DECORATIONS:

1. Decide on color scheme and theme for wedding._____

_____

2. Measure table and chairs to be used for wedding project, calculate yardage required for each project. _____

_____

3. Collect fabric swatches at fabric store for wedding projects. _____

_____

4. Purchase roll paper for pattern making._____

_____

5. Sewing: enlist help from friends and family or hire a seamstress. _____

_____

_____

	Fabric #1	Fabric #2	Fabric #3
Swag Tablecloth			
Yardage			
Notions			
Jabots			
Yardage			
Notions			
Round Tablecloth			
Yardage			
Notions			
Square Tablecloth			
Yardage			
Notions			
Rectangle Tablecloth			
Yardage			
Notions			
Chair Cushions			
Yardage			
Notions			
Placemats			
Yardage			
Notions			
Napkins			
Yardage			
Notions			

Chapter 7

FIVE WEDDING MENUS

Food and beverage is a social experience where body, mind and spirit are all in harmony. One's kitchen, the heart of any home, is a workshop that brings all three elements together in social, sustenance and creativity. As my four children can verify, my kitchen is a special place where works of art originate, impromptu gatherings occur, and fellowship abounds.

These wedding menus have been carefully organized with tested recipes, designed to correspond to a variety of wedding celebration styles and other pre-wedding social events; engagement announcements, showers and rehearsal dinner. Organize an advance tasting of your choice of garden wedding cuisine with friends or family. Recipes can be increased to accommodate your gathering. Asterisk (*) indicates recipes are listed in Chapter 9 Wedding Recipes.

Champagne   Pineapple grapefruit juice
Brunch   * Cappuccino french toast with mocha syrup
9 am to Noon   and vanilla butter
      Strawberries and cantaloupe garnish
      Mild Italian sausage
      Croissants
      * Fresh Strawberry flan
      Green tea
      Champagne

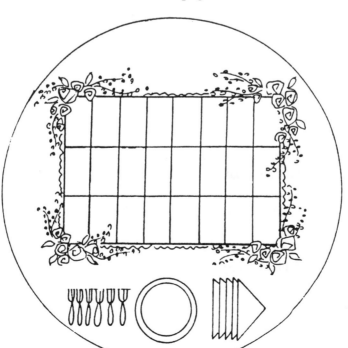

Wedding Cake Table cutting suggestions for one layer rectangular cake.

Verandah
Luncheon
Noon to 2 pm

* Broiled salmon with cucumber/dill sauce
* Assorted baby green salad with raspberry
   dressing
* Minted new potatoes
* Blueberry cream tort
* Spicy iced coffee/Cafe au Lait
* Brides champagne punch

Afternoon
Tea
2 pm to 4 pm

* Dijon sausage rolls
* Tea sandwiches:
      Cream cheese with black walnut,
      chicken salad and cheddar shrimp salad
* Fresh fruit and cream dip
* Balsam mountain angle cake
* Herbal teas and SAVORY iced teas
* Wedding Wine cooler

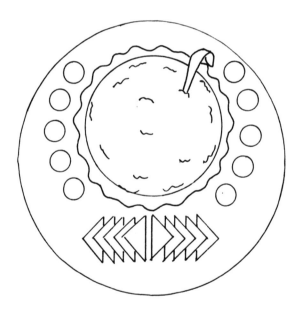

Brides Champagne
Punch Bowl or
Garden Wedding
(Non alcoholic)
Punch Bowl

Garden
Wedding Buffet
4 to 6 pm
(serves 12)

* Mediterranean chicken
   Long grain white rice or wild rice
   Tossed salad
   Crusty rolls
* Crudite's (raw vegetables) with spinach dip
* Black Russian Gateau
   Flavored coffees
* Brides Champagne Punch or Garden Wedding Punch (non-
   alcoholic

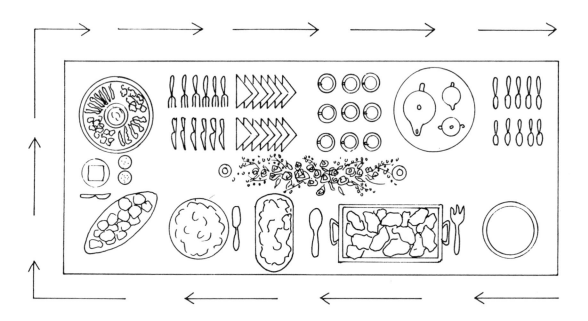

The Buffet Table

A rectangular layout provides for a smooth flow of traffic. If space does not permit for one large table, this arrangement can be divided into two or three smaller serving stations: food, beverage, plates and cutlery.

Twilight   * Cool Lime Cheesecake
Dessert   * Black Cherry Gateau
and Cappuccino   * Linzer Cookies Au Chocolate
7 pm to 9 pm   Assorted cheeses, crackers, red and green grapes
                       Fresh whole strawberries in a bowl
             * Spicy baked nuts
                       Champagne
                       Cappuccino/espresso bar

CHECK LIST FOR WEDDING MENU

Food Preparation Schedule By "Team" Members:

Recipe	Ingredients	Prepared by	Delivery date and time

Chapter 8

BEVERAGE

The Art of Toasting:

Toasting, which has become an accepted part of our social occasions, has it's roots in ancient times. One story has it that the early Christians believed the bell-like sound of the 'clink' would scare away the devil. A logical explanation for toasting is that it brings all five senses into play in order to get the greatest enjoyment from wine. Since wine is judged by it's **color, aroma** and **taste**, the act of **touching** another's glass produces a **sound**, bringing the senses together and increasing the pleasure of a shared experience. Consult your public library or book store for books on wedding toasts.

> *Grow old with me!*
> *The best is yet to be,*
> *The last of life,*
> *For which, the first is made,*
> *Robert Browning*

> *Irish Blessing*

> *May the road rise to meet you.*
> *May the wind be always at your back,*
> *the sun shine warm upon your face,*
> *the rain fall soft upon your fields,*
> *and until we meet again*
> *may God hold you in the palm of His hand*
> *Unknown.*

WINE WISDOM:

The success of the vast Roman Empire can be attributed in part, to wine. Since the great rivers of Europe were Caesar's only access through a vast and hostile population, he clear cut the forests along the valleys and banks and planted grape vines. By doing so he not only gave protection to his advancing legions, but coaxed inhabitants to work the land; a bonus that brought the introduction of wine growing into these regions.

Directing the public relations activities for a Canadian winery was, for me, much like doing post graduate work on this amazing industry. I soon learned that wine is a food product; that in most cultures is consumed with food, before, during or after meals. Drinking wine in moderation can be good for your health. It aids digestion, increases circulation and reduces cholesterol. Wine contains vitamins (A, B1, B6, B12 and C) and trace minerals (calcium, phosphorus, potassium, iron, sodium and magnesium).

Store wine in a dark, cool place the bottles on their sides so the cork is wet at all times, ensuring that no oxidation will take place. After opening, store wine that is not used in the refrigerator. When wine makes contact with the air after opening, oxidation begins and wine deteriorates after one week. Left over wine will add a zest to your cooking.

The popularity of wine coolers in our diet conscious society can be attributed to its low alcohol content. Alcohol provides almost twice as many calories as sugar in a serving of wine. There are 6.9 calories per gram in alcohol, and only 4 calories per gram in sugar. A dry wine with a large amount of alcohol will have more calories than a slightly sweet wine with a very low alcohol content.

White Wine: Should be chilled, but not too cold as it will mask the delicate flavors. Serve dry white wine with fish, poultry, light pasta dishes and delicate cheeses.

Red Wine: Serve room temperature although if the climate or temperature in your home is hot, you may want to quickly chill it. Serve dry red wines with red meat, game, red pasta and robust cheeses.

Blush: Serve chilled with poultry, ham and light foods.

Champagne: Serve chilled in ice, before, during and after meals; excellent with dessert.

Decanting: If fragments of the cork have fallen into the wine bottle or if there is sedimentation in the wine, pour wine into a decanter an hour or so before serving.

Serving wine: Allow two 6 oz. servings of wine per person, one 6 oz. serving of champagne per person, one 4 oz. serving dessert wine per person.

Before meals:	Champagne, dry sherry, vermouth, wine coolers
During meals:	Red, white and blush wines, champagne
Dessert:	Champagne,
After meals:	Champagne, port, cream sherry

Wine suggestions:

White wine:	Riesling, Sauvignon Blanc, Chardonnay
Red wine:	Grenache, Merlot, Shiraz Cabernet
Blush wine:	Zinfandel
Champagne:	Xenius Brut Reserva, Cooks Grande Reserve

Wine servings:

Bottle Size	6 oz Serving
25.6 oz	4
32 oz	5
52 oz magnum	8
104 oz jeroboam	17

| **All Purpose** | **Red Wine** | **Champagne** |

Coffee Culture:

Growing up on New York's Long Island, I learned that the aroma of freshly brewed coffee signalled the arrival of guests and news of the day. It was in the sunny warm kitchen of my childhood, that I began to associate the aroma of freshly brewed coffee with social graces.

Coffee is a fruit, much like the cherry, that grows in temperate climates on a shrub that reach heights of 6 to 30 feet. In the late thirteenth century Eastern legend makes reference to coffee as a food product and stimulant. By the fifteenth century the Turks were known to be experimenting with flavoured coffees, adding cinnamon, cloves and essence. In the mid sixteenth century the popularity of this thick dark beverage resulted in the growth of urban coffee houses in the Mideast, where men gathered to discuss news of the day. When coffee houses began appearing in western Europe, coffee changed in two significant ways; sweetener was added and the drip method of brewing developed instead of boiling the grounds. Instant coffee first made its appearance in the 1850's as a concentrate. Adding hot water produced a cup of coffee.

Coffee contains oils which leave a film that can produce an undesirable flavor in your coffee, if equipment is not cleaned with hot sudsy water and rinsed thoroughly. Use freshly drawn water and freshly ground coffee in the grind appropriate for your coffee maker. Store coffee in the freezer, in an air tight container to preserve its freshness. Serve coffee as soon as possible, after it is brewed.

Coffee for a Crowd

| 1/2 lb coffee | 1 gallon water | 25 servings |
| 1 lb coffee | 2 gallon water | 50 servings |

Tea Traditions:

An appreciation for the delights of tea began for me when I studied and worked in London, England. Our "tea lady" would arrive at 3:30 pm sharp, pushing her cart through the corridors, announcing in a near whisper that tea was served. Work, study and time stopped, and for that moment the world became a gentler place.

Tea is an herb that is grown on plants, bushes and trees. Its origins date back 3,000 years to China and later in India, where it was revered for its curative powers and as a beverage promoting peace and harmony. The ancient Egyptians and Greeks recognized the value of herbs in curing diseases, as a beverage and use in aromatic oils, and cosmetics. Tea, with it's wonderful health giving properties, entered medieval western Europe through the monasteries by traveling monks and pilgrims.

Formal Tea originated in 18th century England as an afternoon break between lunch and a late supper. It soon became an event in itself when dainty sandwiches and cakes were added to "tea time" and eventually replaced lunch. Today, afternoon tea is served between 2 pm and 4 pm, accompanied by an assortment of dainty finger foods. The daily use of herbal tea has grown with our appreciation for healthy lifestyles and, perhaps, for their symbolic meanings.

Chamomile - insight, tolerance	**Dandelion** - prophecy
Hibiscus - elegance	**Lemon** - rejuvenation
Marjoram - joy	**Mint** - warmhearted
Parsley - gaiety,	**Rose** - devotion
Sage - prudence, virtue	

Herbal tea can be purchased loose or in convenient bags at health food stores, specialty stores and beverage section of your grocery store. Listed are some popular blends and simple (one herb) teas.

Earl Grey	China and Darjeeling teas, scented with oil of bergamot. Serve it with or without milk.
English Breakfast	Ceylon and Indian teas have a full-bodied flavor. Taken with milk or lemon.
Darjeeling	This tea is from the foothills of the Himalayas and is served with milk or lemon
Ceylon	Made from broken orange pekoe leaves grown in the hills of SriLanka. Good with milk or lemon or iced.
Green Gunpowder	Traditional Chinese green tea, a weaker delicate straw colored. Drink this tea by itself

Experiment with a variety of beverage recipes listed in Chapter 9 Wedding Recipes before making a selection for your wedding reception.

Bride's Bowl Champagne Punch   Tea preparation for a large gathering
Garden Wedding (non-alcoholic) Punch   Russian Tea
Coffee Preparation for a large gathering   Sun Steeped Iced Tea
Cafe' au Lait   Southern Blush Iced Tea
Cappuccino   Festive Iced Tea Cubes
Turkish Coffee
Irish Coffee

CHECK LIST FOR BEVERAGE:

Wine and Champagne:

Punch recipe:_____

Punch Bowl _____ Punch cups _____

Red wine	Bottle size	Cost per bottle

White wine	Bottle size	Cost per bottle

Blush wine	Bottle size	Cost per bottle

Champagne	Bottle size	Cost per bottle

Delivery date _____ Time _____ Location _____

Does the wine store have a stemware loan with purchase service? _____

Art of Toasting:

Reference material _____

Toast _____ Recipient _____

Toast _____ Recipient _____

Toast _____ Recipient _____

Toast _____ Recipient _____

Coffee:

Variety/Blend _____

Creamer _____

Sweetener _____

Coffee recipes _____

Special equipment (espresso, cappuccino maker) _____

    Tea:

Variety/blends _____

Lemon _____

Sweetener _____

Milk _____

Tea recipes _____

Beverage notes

Chapter 9

WEDDING RECIPES

Wedding Cake

The following carrot nut cake is moist, delicious and suitable for a wedding cake baked in round or square tiers or rectangular shape. It can be exchanged with any dessert recipes in the other Wedding Menus. Decorate your wedding cake with fresh flowers: pansies, roses, nasturtiums or silk flowers. Visit the cake decorating section of your local arts and craft store for wedding cake decorating ideas.

CARROT NUT CAKE

2 cups all purpose flour	2 tsp. baking powder
1 tsp. baking soda	1 tsp. salt
2 tsp. cinnamon	2 cup granulated sugar
1 cup vegetable oil	4 eggs
3 cups finely grated raw carrots	1 cup finely chopped walnuts

Combine flour, baking powder, baking soda, salt and cinnamon in a bowl. In a large beater bowl, blend sugar and oil.   Beat in eggs until mixture is smooth and fluffy. Gradually stir in the dry ingredients until thoroughly combined. Stir in the grated carrots and chopped nuts to blend. Pour an equal amount into a prepared 9" x 13" pan (line bottom with greased wax paper). Bake at 325 deg. F. about 60 minutes or until cake springs back when lightly touched. Cool 20 minutes before removing from pan.

CREAM CHEESE FROSTING

One 8 oz. pkg. white cream cheese	3 tbsp. oil
4 cups icing sugar	1/4 tsp. salt
Yellow food coloring	

Beat cream cheese and oil. Gradually add icing sugar and salt. Beat until smooth. Add a few drops yellow food coloring. Beat until blended. Arrange paper doilies on a serving tray; carefully transfer the cake onto the doilies. Spread cream cheese frosting on top and sides of cake. Decorate your Carrot Nut Wedding Cake with edible fresh flowers (roses, pansies or nasturtiums) silk flowers or sugared fruit.

Toasting the Bride and Groom

The following wedding punch recipes can be offered before, during or after eating or simply as a means to toast the bride and groom. Serve to guests in champagne flute glasses on a tray or self serve from a punch bowl table.

BRIDES CHAMPAGNE PUNCH
(14 - 4 oz. Servings)

2 cups seasonal fruit: sliced orange, lemon, star fruit, pineapple strawberries, pitted cherries
Ice

1- 750 ml. bottle white wine, chilled
1- 750 ml. bottle champagne, chilled
4 oz. brandy

Add fruit, ice, white wine and brandy to a punch bowl. Just before serving add the champagne.

GARDEN WEDDING (non-alcoholic) PUNCH
(about 40- 4 oz. servings)
Melody Dawn Smith, Los Angeles

64 oz. (2 quarts) gingerale
64 oz. (2 quarts) orange juice
Ice

48 oz. cranberry cocktail juice
2 oranges, sliced thinly

Combine juices and ice in a large punch bowl. Just before serving add the gingerale and float orange slices on top.

WEDDING WINE COOLER

Pour 2 oz. (1/4 cup) blush wine into each champagne flute glass. Add ice, fill with soda water and garnish with a lemon twist. Serve Wedding Wine Cooler to guests on a tray or prepare while they wait at your beverage table.

Champagne Brunch

CAPPUCCINO FRENCH TOAST with VANILLA BUTTER and MOCHA SYRUP
(serves 6)

8 large eggs
1 cup * mocha syrup

3 cups milk
1 loaf french bread

In a large bowl, beat eggs, gradually adding milk, then mocha syrup. Slice twelve, one inch diagonal pieces of french bread. Place into one or two large, shallow dishes. Pour cappuccino custard over the bread, cover and chill for half an hour until custard is absorbed. Melt butter or margarine in a large skillet. When skillet is hot, place the bread slices in and cook slowly for 10 minutes, turn and cook another 10 minutes or until custard is set. Keep cooked french toast in a warming oven until remaining bread slices are cooked.

MOCHA SYRUP
(yield: 2-1/4 cups)

3/4 cup strong coffee, or add 3 tablespoons instant coffee to 3/4 cup boiling water
3 tsp. cocoa powder

3/4 cup corn syrup
1-1/2 cups brown sugar

Add all ingredients to a medium saucepan, stir over medium-high heat until it reaches a boil, reduce heat to low and simmer 3 to 4 minutes, stirring until sugar is dissolved and syrup has thickened. Remove from heat. This syrup can be made in advance and stored in the refrigerator until ready to use.

VANILLA BUTTER

2/3 cup butter, room temperature   2 cups confectioners' sugar, sifted
1 tsp. vanilla

Cream butter, gradually add the sugar beating until the consistency of whipped cream. Add vanilla drop by drop. Store in refrigerator. Can be made a day in advance. Serve at room temperature.

CAPPUCCINO FRENCH TOAST ASSEMBLY:

Place two slices of Cappuccino French Toast on pre-warmed plates. Drizzle mocha syrup over each and top with a teaspoon of vanilla butter, (and one shake of cinnamon if desired) Garnish the side of the plate with blueberries and thin crescents of cantaloupe. Serve with mild Italian sausage.

STRAWBERRY FLAN

(serves 8)

This beautiful dessert is a treasure that my maternal grandmother, Helena Hammer Retz, brought with her to the "new world" as a young bride. Nana prepared this dessert using whatever fruit was in season, or in winter, canned peaches. It can be served with or without the whipped cream and toasted almonds.

ASSEMBLY

Pour the pudding into the flan well, arrange strawberries in circles within circles with one perfect berry at the center. Spoon glaze over each berry until all are covered. Whipped cream and toasted almonds can be added to individual servings or spooned over the outer edge of the flan (sprinkle with almonds).

FLAN

1-1/3 cup cake flour   2 tsp. baking powder
1/4 tsp. salt   1/4 cup butter
3/4 cup sugar   ½ tsp. vanilla
1 farm fresh egg   1/4 cup milk

Sift flour, baking powder and salt together. Cream butter, gradually adding sugar, vanilla and egg. Add flour and milk alternately. This will be a firm batter. Pour into a buttered and floured 11" flan pan. Bake at 350 deg. F for 15 to 20 minutes or until center springs up when lightly touched. Cool on a wire rack, remove from flan pan and transfer to cake plate. Flan can be frozen until needed.

STRAWBERRIES

Wash and hull and halve one pint medium size strawberries (reserve one perfect strawberry with stem and leaves in tact for the center of the flan). To speed up the assembly of berries on the flan, pre-arrange the fruit on a plate with the same diameter as the center of the flan, them simply transfer the strawberries to the flan.

PUDDING

1 cup milk   1-1/2 tbsp. cornstarch
2 tbsp. sugar   1/8 tsp. salt
½ tsp vanilla

In top of a double boiler, mix sugar, cornstarch and salt. Add 1/4 cup milk and stir until smooth: add remainder of milk, stirring until smooth. Cook over hot water stirring constantly until pudding thickens. Continue stirring for another 5 minutes, add vanilla and cool, but do not let set. Pour into the flan well. This pudding can be made in advance and refrigerated in air tight container until needed. Turn into a saucepan and stir vigorously warm slowly to regain smooth texture.

GLAZE

Use Oetker clear glaze (available in the baking section of your local grocery store). Prepare according to package directions. Spoon over fruit until all is covered. If Oetker is not available in your area, apple jelly can be used. Warm ½ cup apple jelly in a sauce pan over low heat. Allow to cool slightly but not set before spooning over fruit.

TOASTED ALMONDS

Spread ½ cup slivered almonds on a cookie sheet, bake at 300 deg. F for 10 minutes or until golden brown. Keep an eye on the almonds as they will scorch very quickly.

WHIPPED CREAM

½ pint whipping cream   3 tbsp. icing sugar
½ tsp. vanilla   Pinch of salt

In a small beater bowl, beat the whipped cream until it begins to thicken; add sugar, salt and vanilla. Continue beating until forms soft peaks. Do not over beat or you will have butter.

Verandah Luncheon

BROILED SALMON STEAKS WITH CUCUMBER-DILL SAUCE
(serves 8)

8 fresh salmon steaks   2 lemons cut into wedges
Salt, pepper, lemon juice

Rinse salmon steaks, pat dry with paper towels.   Season with salt, pepper and lemon juice. Dot each steak with butter and place on a broiler shelf and cook 8 to 10 minutes. Turn the salmon steaks over and season with salt, pepper, lemon juice and dot of butter. Grill until flesh shrinks from the bone. Place each salmon steak on warmed plates, garnish with hot cucumber-dill sauce and a lemon wedge.

CUCUMBER-DILL SAUCE

½ cup butter   1 English cucumber, peeled and diced
1 cup all purpose flour   2 ½ cups chicken stock
1/3 cup snipped fresh dill   2/3 cup sour cream

Melt butter, saute cucumber for one minute, remove from heat, stir in flour. Blend in chicken stock and return to heat, bringing to a low boil. Add dill and simmer for 3 minutes stirring constantly. Remove from heat and add sour cream. Season to taste with salt and pepper.

Store the Cucumber-Dill Sauce in the refrigerator until ready to use. Serve hot over salmon steaks or a fine salmon loaf.

MINTED NEW POTATOES

New potatoes in themselves are as tender as peas. The green grocer where I shopped while living in London England, suggested adding a sprig of fresh mint while cooking. The flavor is delicate and simply elegant. Select new potatoes 1" in diameter, allowing four to five per person. Scrub and place in saucepan with sprigs of fresh mint. Cook until fork tender, drain and remove mint.

ASSORTED BABY GREEN SALAD with RASPBERRY DRESSING
(serves 8)
Melody Dawn Smith, Los Angeles

One 5 oz. bag baby salad greens	1/3 cup fresh raspberries
1/4 cup crumbled blue cheese	1/3 cup pistachio nuts
1 small red onion, sliced thinly	1 bottle raspberry vinaigrette dressing

Rinse salad greens and pat dry with paper towels. Break into bite size pieces and transfer into salad bowl. Sprinkle with pistachio nuts, blue cheese, red onions. When ready to serve toss with raspberry vinaigrette dressing.

BLUEBERRY CREAM TORTE
(serves 8 -10)

This lovely dessert was served to me at Afternoon Tea by the ministers wife at the church I attended while living in London, England. Mrs Evelyn Crompton generously supplied me with this recipe.

Bake the shortbread crust in a 9" spring form pan, cool; then pour in the previously cooled blueberry filling, top with sour cream toping and bake at 350 deg. F for 45 minutes. Cool once more, then chill before removing from the spring form pan.

SHORTBREAD CRUST

3/4 cup butter	1/4 cup granulated sugar
2 fresh eggs yolks	2 cups all purpose flour
1 tsp. baking powder	½ tsp. salt

Cream butter and sugar. Add egg yolks and beat until fluffy. Mix together: flour, baking powder and salt. Blend into creamed mixture. Press 2/3 of dough into the bottom of a 9" spring form pan. Bake at 400 deg. F for 10 minutes, cool. Reduce oven temperature to 350 deg. F, press remaining dough 1-1/2" up sides of pan. Fill with blueberry filling, then cover with sour cream toping. Bake at 350 deg. F for 45 minutes. Cool and chill before removing from spring form pan.

BLUEBERRY FILLING

4 cups fresh blueberries	1/4 cup quick-cooking tapioca
½ tsp. cinnamon	1/8 tsp. nutmeg
½ cup granulated sugar	1 cup water
½ tsp. grated lemon	2 tbsp. cornstarch

In a medium sauce pan, combine blueberries, sugar, tapioca, lemon gratings and spices. Let stand 15 minutes. Cook and stir until bubbly. Cool, then turn into shortbread crust.

SOUR CREAM TOPPING

2 slightly beaten egg yolks   2 cups sour cream
½ cup sugar   1 tsp. vanilla

Mix vigorously; 2 slightly beaten egg yolks, sour cream, sugar and vanilla until smooth and sugar is dissolved. Spoon evenly over the blueberry filling. Bake at 350 deg. F for 45 minutes.

* Cooking tip: Freeze your egg whites in an 10 oz container. When this container is filled, you will have enough for the Balsam Mountain Angle Cake, (Recipe is given in the Afternoon Tea section). Nothing beats the delicate flavor and texture of a fresh baked angle food cake.

SPICY ICED COFFEE
(refer to beverage recipes at the end to this chapter)

Afternoon Tea

DIJON SAUSAGE ROLLS
(3 to 4 - 1" sausage rolls)

1 lb. frozen beef sausage   1 package pie crust mix
2 tbsp. chopped parsley   1 jar Dijon mustard
1 egg, beaten

Parboil sausages 5 to 10 minuted, drain on paper towels, cool. Prepare pie crust according to package directions. Roll out pastry into two rectangles, wide enough to wrap around a sausage and long enough to line up all the sausages end to end. Spread Dijon mustard along the longest edge of both pastry rectangles, sprinkle with parsley. Line up the sausages end to end, fold over the pie curst, seal with seam at bottom. Brush pastry roll with beaten egg. This creates a lovely golden glaze. Cut sausage roll into one inch pieces, place on a baking sheet. Bake at 400 deg. F for 10 to 15 minutes. Reduce heat if sausage rolls are browning too quickly. Serve hot or cold.

TEA SANDWICHES

Use day old bread, sliced thin. Store in the refrigerator so that it will be firm and easy to spread. A two pound loaf of bread, thinly sliced, should yield bout 40 slices (20 sandwiches cut into 80 bite size tea sandwiches). Allow one to two whole sandwiches per person (three for men). Cut off crusts before using one of the following spreads. Apply the spread thinly to only one slice of bread for each tea sandwich. Cover the entire surface to the edges and corners. Close with the other slice of bread and press firmly. Store in the refrigerator until ready to serve. Cut into bars or diagonally.

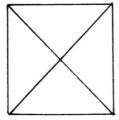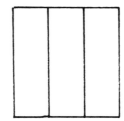

CREAM CHEESE and BLACK WALNUT

1 lb. cream cheese, room temperature   1 cup chopped walnuts
Sourdough Bread

Beat cream cheese until soft, moisten with cream or milk. Add chopped walnuts. Remove crust from bread. Spread on sourdough bread slices, firmly place on the top slice. Refrigerate in air tight container. When ready to serve, cut into triangles or bars.

CHICKEN SALAD

Pumpernickel bread   3 tbsp. mayonnaise
1 cup cooked chicken, cubed   2 slices crisp bacon
1/4 tsp salt

Put all ingredients in blender; buzz until smooth. Stop blender during blending and push ingredients toward blades with a rubber spatula (yield 1 cup, enough for 30 slices of bread). Spread on slices of bread and cut into bite size shapes.

CHEDDAR - SHRIMP SPREAD

1 tbsp. milk   ½ cup mayonnaise
1/4 pound cheddar cheese, cubed   ½ cup cooked clean shrimp fresh or
                                                       canned
2 drops tobasco sauce   1/4 of a small onion
Whole wheat bread

Put all ingredients in a blender, cover and blend until smooth. Stop blender and push ingredients toward blades with rubber spatula. (yield 1 ½ cups, enough for 40 slices of bread)
  Remove crusts, cut 2" rounds with a cookie cutter. Spread thinly on rounds, garnish this canape (open faced sandwich) with fresh sniped parsley or sprinkle with paprika.

FRESH FRUIT and CREAM DIP

1 egg slightly beaten   2 tbsp. flour
1/3 cup sugar   ½ cup pineapple juice
1 orange   1 lemon
½ pint whipping cream

In a double boiler add: egg, sugar, flour and the juice of ½ the lemon and ½ the orange and

½ cup pineapple juice. Cook until thick, cool. In a small beater bowl, beat the whipping cream until it forms soft peaks, fold into the cooled cream dip mixture.

ASSEMBLY:

Pour cream dip into a bowl place in the center of a plate, surrounded by bite sized fruit: pears, bananas, pineapple titbits, watermelon bits, cantaloupe, strawberries, cherries. Place a container of picks to spear the fruit.

BALSAM MOUNTAIN ANGLE CAKE
(serves 8-10)
Gene Sweisberger, Fort Myers, Florida

Mary Rose Sweisberger was renown in South Bend, Indiana for her angle food cake. Her son Gene has taken it one step further with his exquisite decorating treatment.

ANGLE CAKE

8 oz. egg whites (8 or more)	1/4 tsp. salt
1 tsp. cream of tartar	½ tsp coconut extract
1 tsp. vanilla	1 1/4 cup granulated sugar
1 cup cake and pastry flour	

Beat egg whites until foamy, add cream of tartar, continue beating until form soft peaks. Add coconut extract and vanilla. Sift flour and sugar, fold carefully with a spatula into the beaten whites one tablespoon at a time. Spoon into a 10" tube pan that has been dusted with flour (do not butter the pan).Bake at 325 deg. F for 50 minutes. Turn off the oven and let cake remain in oven another 10 minutes longer. Remove cake from oven and turn upside down (resting center on a funnel or narrow neck bottle) so that cake is hanging while it cools for at least one hour. Gently slip a sharp knife around the edges of the tube pan to release. Angle cake improves with age. Make this at least a day before needed.

ASSEMBLY:

16 oz. jar lemon curd	½ pint whipping cream
3 tbsp. icing sugar	2 tsp. gelatin

Fresh picked yellow, purple and white
pansies, rinsed and towel dried.

In a bowl, add whipped cream, stir in gelatin and beat until the cream forms oft peaks. Do not over beat as the result will be butter. Split the angle cake horizontally so that you have 3 layers. Place first layer on a cake plate, spread with lemon curd, arrange a few pansies on top. Place second layer on top and spread with lemon curd, place pansies on top. Place third layer on top. Spread with whipped cream frosting, decorate top and sides with pansies.

HERBAL TEA AND SAVORY ICED TEA
(refer to beverage recipes at the end of this chapter)

Garden Wedding Buffet

MEDITERRANEAN CHICKEN
(serves 8)

8 chicken breasts, about 4 oz each, skins removed
2-3 cloves of garlic, crushed
1/4 tsp. marjoram
½ pint chicken stock
Salt and pepper to taste

4 slices of bacon cut into 1" pieces
4 onions, sliced
2 green peppers, sliced thickly
1 -14 oz. can whole tomatoes
1/4 cup olive oil

In a heavy sauce pan, cook bacon until golden. Remove and set aside. Add olive oil and chicken pieces, browning on both sides. Place browned chicken pieces into a shallow baking dish. Saute onions until soft, add green peppers, garlic, marjoram, salt and pepper and simmer for 10 minutes, covered. Add tomatoes and chicken stock. Ladle the vegetables over the chicken. Bake at 350 deg. F for 40 minutes. Serve over white long grain rice or wild rice.

CRUDITE'S (raw vegetables) WITH SPINACH DIP
(serves 12)
Melody Dawn Smith, Los Angeles

carrot sticks
cucumbers
broccoli
mushrooms
radish

celery
green and red peppers
cauliflower
cherry tomatoes
turnip

Select four or five vegetables from the above list in a variety of colors. Wash, peel and cut into bite size pieces. Store in the refrigerator in air tight containers or zip lock bags until ready to use.

Arrange attractively into a serving dish or tray with dipping dish at the center.
SPINACH DIP

1 small package frozen spinach
16 oz container sour cream

1 envelope Knorr cream of leak soup

Thaw spinach and drain, squeeze excess water out by placing between paper towels. Combine sour cream, soup mix and spinach and store in an air tight container. Prepare 12 to 24 hours before serving so that flavors can blend.

BLACK RUSSIAN TORT
(serves 8-10)
Mary Etta Burr and the Boundry Street Gang, Waynesville NC

1 box devils food cake mix
1 cup cooking oil
1/4 cup vodka
½ cup water

1 small pkg. chocolate instant pudding
4 eggs
½ cup Kahlua

Mix dry ingredients together in a beater bowl. Add eggs, oil vodka, Kahlua and water. Beat 4 minutes until smooth. Pour into a greased and floured bundt cake pan. Bake at 350 deg. F for 50 minutes.

BLACK RUSSIAN GLAZE

1 cup semi sweet chocolate chips

1/4 Kahlua

1 tbsp. vodka

1 tbsp vegetable oil

While cake is still warm, drizzle glaze from center to sides until surface is covered with a zig zag pattern. In a double boiler, combine ingredients, heat and stir until melted and smooth.

Twilight Dessert and coffee

COOL LIME CHEESECAKE
(serves 10-12)
Ann Marie Brunner, London, Canada
SHORTBREAD CRUST

3 cups all purpose flour

1 farm fresh egg

½ lb. butter

1/4 cup sugar

Cut butter into flour and sugar until the size of peas. Add egg and mix into a soft dough. Line the bottom of a 10" spring form pan that has been greased and lined with wax paper. Bake at 400 deg. F for 10 minutes. Cool.

COOL LIME FILLING

1 envelope unflavored gelatin

½ cup granulated sugar

1/3 cup white rum

½ cup lime juice

1 tsp. grated lemon rind

1 tsp. grated lime rind

4 eggs separated

1 lb. cream cheese

½ cup icing sugar

½ pint whipping cream

In a double boiler add: gelatin, sugar, rum and lime juice. Cook and stir until sugar dissolves. Add lime and lemon rind and egg yolks stirring constantly until custard thickens. Cool. Beat cream cheese until light and smooth. Add cooled gelatin mixture, blending well. In separate mixing bowls, beat whipping cream and icing sugar. In the second bowl, beat egg whites until stiff. Fold all ingredients into cream cheese, gelatin mixture. Pour into the spring form pan with the cooled, baked crust shell. Chill for 12 hours.

BLACK CHERRY GATEAU
(Makes one 11" gateau, serves 8)
PASTRY

1 cup butter, room temperature

1-2/3 cups flour

1 cup sugar

3 egg yolks

1 egg white

1 egg yolk, beaten (glaze for crust)

1 tbsp. white rum

32 oz. best quality black cherry jam
(Polaner jam is recommended)

This exquisite dessert can be found in gourmet or European bakeries. It has a delicate, flavorful and flaky pastry. The gateau requires an 11" flan ring with a removable bottom. Blend flour and sugar together. Beat butter until smooth, add flour mixture, 3 egg yolks, 1 egg white and rum. Mix well, knead lightly and form into a ball. Wrap in plastic and refrigerate for half an hour or until firm. Avoid over handling this pastry, as the end result will be tough and not be flaky. Roll out 2/3 of the pastry into a circle about 1/2" thick, large enough to line the flan ring and up the sides. Place pastry into the flan ring, gently working it up the sides. Brush the edge with beaten egg yolk so the top will seal well. Pour in the black cherry preserve. Roll out the remaining 1/3 pastry into a circle and cover the top, trim off surplus pastry, crimp edges and score the top with a fork or knife so steam can escape. Brush egg yolk over the top for a golden finish. Place on a baking sheet and bake at 350 deg. F for 35 minutes. When baked, remove only the outer flan ring and allow to cool on the baking sheet until it is firm enough to move, then cool on a wire rack. The gateau can be made in advance and frozen until needed. Thaw overnight in the refrigerator.

LINZER COOKIES AU CHOCOLATE
(2 ½ to 3 dozen 2 ½ "cookies)

2-1/3 cups flour	½ tsp. vanilla extract
1 tsp. baking powder	½ tsp. cinnamon
1/4 tsp. nutmeg	½ tsp. salt
1 cup butter, room temperature	1 cup granulated sugar
2 farm fresh eggs	1 cup best quality raspberry preserve
1 tsp. lemon juice	2 cups semi sweet chocolate chips
1 tbsp. vegetable oil	

These splendid cookies have been a favorite of mine since first introduced to them in France years ago. They are available in gourmet and European bakeries. You will need a cookie or donut cutter with a removable center ring to make this sandwich style cookie. For best results use the freshest and best ingredients. In a separate bowl, combine: flour, baking powder, cinnamon, nutmeg, salt. In a large bowl, beat butter and sugar until creamy, add eggs and vanilla. Gradually add dry ingredients until form a soft dough. Divide into two balls, wrap individually and refrigerate until firm. On a floured surface, roll out dough to a 1/8" thickness. Cut an equal amount of bottom (solid) rounds and hole-in-the-center rounds. Bake on ungreased cookie sheets at 350 deg. F for 8 to 10 minutes. Cool on a wire rack. In a double boiler on medium heat, melt the chocolate chips and oil stirring until smooth. Spread a thin layer of chocolate on each bottom solid round. Place raspberry preserve and 1 tsp. lemon juice in a small saucepan and melt over low heat. Drop a level teaspoon of raspberry preserve onto the center of the chocolate layered bottoms. Place cookie with hole-in-the-center on top to complete the sandwich.

SPICY BAKED NUTS
(yield 4 lbs.)
Shirley Savigny, London, Canada

1 lb raw, blanched and unsalted:	½ tsp salt

almonds, cashews, filberts, peanuts

2 tsp. ginger

1 tsp. allspice

2 tsp. cinnamon

1 tsp. cloves

1 cup raisins

1 ½ cups granulated sugar

4 egg whites

Place nuts on a baking sheet and roast at 250 deg. F until light golden color, stirring frequently, about ½ hour. Cool. Mix sugar with spices. Beat egg whites lightly. Place nuts into a sieve that fits into the bowl containing egg whites.. Drop nuts and raisins a few at a time into the egg whites. Remove and coat nuts and raisins liberally with the sugar and spices, stirring together. Sprinkle sugar and spice onto a baking sheet. Spread spiced nuts and raisins on the baking sheet. Bake at 200 deg. F for 2 ½ hours, stirring frequently. Cool and store in an air tight container until ready to use.

* For convenience, lease a cappuccino or espresso coffee machine or serve a selection of flavored coffees with the Twilight Dessert.

BEVERAGE RECIPES

Coffee:

CAFE' AU LAIT
(16-6 oz. Servings)

Prepare strong coffee, using 1 ½ cups ground coffee and 6 cups water. Heat 6 cups milk. Pour equal amounts of hot strong coffee and hot milk simultaneously from separate pots into each cup.

IRISH COFFEE
(8 cups)

1 cup chilled whipping cream

1/4 cup icing sugar

1 tsp. vanilla

10 oz. or 1-1/4 cup Irish whisky or

8 tsp. granulated sugar

brandy

Beat whipping cream, vanilla and icing sugar until form soft peaks. Set aside. To each coffee cup, add 2 tbsp. whisky and 1 tsp. granulated sugar; stir while pouring hot coffee into each cup. Top with whipped cream; serve immediately.

TURKISH COFFEE
(4 cups)

4 cups water

1/3 cup granulated sugar

One 3" cinnamon stick

½ cup Turkish-style coffee

Measure water into heavy saucepan. Add sugar and cinnamon and bring to a boil. Stir in coffee, bring to a full boil. Allow brew to froth up three times, then remove from heat. Spoon some of the foam into each cup and ladle coffee over foam.

CAPPUCCINO
(8- 6 oz servings)

2 cups hot water
1 cup dry instant coffee
4 cups strong hot coffee
Chocolate curls

1/4 cup sugar
1/4 tsp. nutmeg
Cream

Stir water and dry instant coffee and cream together. Mix in strong, hot coffee, sugar and nutmeg. Pour into cups and garnish with chocolate curls.

SPICY ICED COFFEE
(8- 8 oz. glasses)

1 stick cinnamon
17 whole cloves
1 cup icing sugar

½ cup ground coffee
9 cups boiling water
½ pint whipping cream

Beat whipping cream in beater bowl, add icing sugar, set aside. Mix cinnamon and cloves with coffee and brew in automatic coffee maker. Add icing sugar to brewed coffee, dissolving completely. Add crushed ice to 8 tall glasses, pour in coffee. Place a scoop of whipped cream in each glass and garnish with powdered cinnamon.

COFFEE ICE CUBES

Freeze freshly brewed, regular-strength coffee in ice cube trays. Place a whole coffee bean in each cube. Freeze no longer than 24 hours as it will loose its flavor and strength. Pour freshly brewed regular-strength coffee over coffee ice cubes in a tall glass or large pitcher. Serve with sweetener and cream or whipped cream.

Tea:

RUSSIAN TEA
(yield 3 gallons - drink hot or cold)
Susan Sorrells, Canton, NC

10 tea bags (Earl Grey or English Breakfast)
Juice from 6 lemons (or 1 ½ cups
Lemon concentrate)
Juice from 12 oranges
(or 1 small can frozen orange juice)

16 cups boiling water
Second amount 16 cups boiling water
4 tsp. whole cloves
4 cups granulated sugar
2 - 48 oz. cans pineapple juice

To a very large container, add the first 16 cups boiling water to tea bags, allow to steep (brew) for 15 minutes. Remove tea bags. Add sugar, cloves and the second 16 cups of boiling water. Let set for 2 hours, then remove the cloves and add fruit juices. Store in the refrigerator or freezer until ready to use.

SOUTHERN BLUSH ICED TEA
Eva Bishop, Waynesville NC

To a 16 oz. Glass add; * Festive Ice Cubes, 1 ½ cup plain iced tea and ½ cup grape juice or cranberry juice. Add sweetener to taste and garnish with a sliced orange.

FESTIVE ICED TEA CUBES

Pour freshly steeped, cooled tea into ice cube trays. Into each cube, place a fresh mint leaf or rose petal, freeze. Remove festive iced tea cubes from trays and place into each glass , pour in the iced tea.

SUN STEEPED ICED TEA
(yield 1 gallon)

1 gallon jug filled with freshly drawn water   4 Constant Comment tea bags
1 cinnamon stick   1/4 tsp nutmeg
Juice and grated rind of 2 lemons and 2 oranges   sugar to taste

Mix ingredients together and pour into a 1 gallon jug. Cap the jug securely and set in the sun for two days. Shake the mixture each 10 to 12 hours. Strain and refrigerate. Serve with festive iced tea cubes.

PLAIN ICED TEA

Pour boiling water over four tea bags, steep 7 to 10 minutes, remove tea bags and sweeten with honey if desired, then refrigerate.

Additional Recipes

Chapter 10

STATIONERY*INVITATIONS*NEWSLETTER

Not only do wedding invitations announce the event but also the style of your wedding (formal, informal, casual). Compose an announcement stating the event, names, date, time and location, including your phone number and a date when a reply is expected. Choose wording that applies to the formality of your wedding. For example, a parent hosted wedding, the invitation includes the name of bride's parent(s) or step parents. If parents are divorced and remarried, state the name of the parent (and spouse if remarried) hosting the wedding. In some cultures the names of the parents of bride and groom are included. Although invitations are traditionally written in third person with a standard format, you can be as creative as you wish. Have several people read your 'proofs' before they are printed.

Parent hosted invitation	**Bride and groom hosted invitation**
Mr & Mrs (first name) (last name)	Ms. (first, middle and last name)
request the honor of your presence	and
at the marriage of (their) (her) (his) daughter	Mr. (first, middle and last name)
(bride's first, middle and last name)	request the honor of your presence
to	at their marriage
(groom's first, middle and last name)	on (day, date, month)
on (day, date and month)	(year spelled out)
(year spelled out)	at (time spelled out)
(time spelled out; a.m. or p.m.)	(ceremony location)
(ceremony location)	(city and state)
(city, state)	

*include reply card stating date when a reply will be appreciated.

* include reply card or your telephone number stating when a reply will be appreciated.

Shop for wedding invitations at print shops, stationery shops or department stores. Order invitations at least three months in advance and mail them four to six weeks before the wedding; one invitation per family and one for single guests. Ask your supplier for envelopes in advance so that you can begin addressing. Purchase thank you notes at this time.

Computer generated invitations: This form of wedding invitation is personalized and creative. Its charm is that you can include a poem or favorite verse in the message. Office supply stores have stationary with or without attractive borders (and matching envelopes) on which your message can be overprinted. Be sure to include all the necessary details; event, names, date, time and location, adding a reply card or your phone number and date when a reply is expected. Mail these invitations four to six weeks before the wedding. To streamline your budget, fax or email your computer generated wedding invitation stating when a telephone reply will be appreciated.

Thank you notes:
Acknowledge wedding gifts soon after they arrive, with a hand written thank you note, expressing appreciation to the giver for the gift and where you will use it. Remember that love, time and thoughtfulness went into the selection of this gift for you. If the gift is money, do not state the amount, only what you plan to purchase with it. The following is a sample thank you note.

Dear _____

Your wonderful gift arrived today. Imagine our delight when we opened the package and discovered this lovely _____ (describe the gift received, why you appreciate it and where it will be used). It is just what we needed for our home. Thank you for your thoughtfulness. _____ and I will think of you fondly each time we have occasion to use the _____.

Kindest regards,

Pre-wedding newsletter: Compose a lighthearted pre-wedding newsletter, announcing details of your wedding, date, place and time. This informal pre-announcement will enable your out-of-town guests to make arrangements for time off work and travel plans. Imagine their anticipation of a combined mini-vacation and wedding! Mention that you will be sending a package with information on travel, accommodations, local attractions and events in your area after you hear from them. Mail, fax or email the newsletter. Refer to Check List for Stationery/Invitations/Newsletter at the end of this chapter detailing the "Things-to-do" folder. The following sample newsletter is a guide for your convenience.

Dear _____

Because our friends and family are dear to our hearts, we want you to be the first to share our wonderful news; _____ and I plan to be married (detail). This will take place on (day, month, year, time, location, city and state). We are so happy and quite busy making plans for a wonderful celebration (detail). Please call us at (phone number) so that we can go into more detail on the events that we have planned.

Since everyone has such busy lives, we trust that the advance notice will enable you to make travel plans and book time off work. Our (town) is especially beautiful at the time of year our wedding is planned (describe). We are preparing a "Things-to-do" folder so that our out-of-town guests are aware of other events and activities to enjoy while visiting our area.

Our wedding will not be complete without you.

Kindest regards,

Organization:
Create a file card for every guest invited. Record name, address, phone, date sent, date invitation accepted, gift received, date thank you note sent. Arrange this information alphabetically into a file box and keep it up to date. Place a guest book on a table at the entrance to your wedding reception. On the signature pages remaining blank, mount candid photos with clever captions.

CHECK LIST FOR STATIONERY/INVITATIONS/NEWSLETTER:

Wedding invitations:
Brides parents _____ Grooms parents _____
Bride and Groom _____ Wedding; Day _____
Date _____ Month _____ Year _____ Time _____
Location; City _____ State _____
Your phone number _____ Date a reply is expected _____
Address where reply is sent _____
Date proofs ready for approval _____ Delivery date _____
Thank you notes _____
Envelopes in advance (to begin addressing) _____
Stationery supplier _____
Address _____
Contact person _____ Phone_____
Total cost _____ Deposit _____ Payment schedule _____
Cancellation policy _____

"Things-to-do" folder:
Area map including wedding activity locations (tracing or photo copy of a map) _____
Affordable accommodations _____ Rates _____
Best highway route to wedding site _____
Train, plane or bus _____ Terminal _____
Schedule _____ Fees _____
Car rental agency _____ Seasonal climate on wedding date _____
Information and brochures for: Local attractions _____ Shopping _____
Leisure activities _____ Festivals _____ Restaurants _____
Children's activities _____ Live music _____ Dancing _____
Names of reliable: Babysitters _____ Health care facility _____

Organization:
File box for guest record keeping _____ Index cards_____ Guest book registry _____

Chapter 11

PHOTOGRAPHER/VIDEOGRAPHER:

PHOTOGRAPHER:

Ask family and trusted friends for recommendations. Examine the photographers previous wedding assignments. Record the name of the photographer assigned to your event to be certain he/she is the same one whose work you have viewed, as the quality of work varies from one photographer to another. Ask the photographer to visit the ceremony and reception site so that he/she will bring all the necessary equipment for the event. Inform your photographer of any restrictions on photography at the house of worship during the ceremony. Ask for and research his/her references and Better Business rating.

Assign a "team" member to work with your photographer at the ceremony and reception. List significant family members, friends, guests and moments to capture. For interesting candid photos distribute some Kodak's single-use cameras on guests tables with a note inviting them to take candid photos and deposit the camera in a basket at the door when they leave. You will be pleasantly surprised when you process this film. These cameras are attractively packaged and cost about $10 each.

VIDEOGRAPHER:

My future son-in-law said that he saw old home movies of his grandparents when they were young and strong and beautiful. It took his breath away. Wedding videos are much like viewing your own wedding as a guest and savoring every moment now and forever.

Interview several videographers before making your final selection. Look at video samples of their work. Record the name of the videographer assigned to your event to be certain he/she is the same on whose work you have reviewed. The quality of work varies from one technician to another. Inform your Videographer of any filming restrictions at the house of worship during the ceremony. A visit to the ceremony and reception site will allow your technician to assess the situation and bring all necessary equipment. Ask for and research references and Better Business rating. Assign a 'team' member to work with your Videographer at the ceremony and reception. List important family members, special friends and guests and moments not to miss.

CHECK LIST FOR PHOTOGRAPHER AND VIDEOGRAPHER

Photographer:
Confirm that your date is available _____ Arrival time _____ Departure time _____
Special equipment needed _____ Backup equipment _____
Is there a limit on film? _____ Does price include finished album? _____
Delivery date of finished product _____
Who owns proofs and negatives _____ Costs for extra photos _____
"Team" member assistant _____ Phone _____
Significant family members _____ Friends _____ Guests _____
Special effects _____ Formal shots _____ Moments to capture _____
Company name _____
Name of photographer assigned to your event _____
Address _____ Phone _____
Total cost _____ Deposit _____ Payment schedule _____
Cancellation policy _____
Disposable cameras _____

Videographer:
Confirm that your date is available _____ Arrival time _____ Departure time _____
Formal shots _____ Moments to capture _____
Significant family members _____ Friends _____ Guests _____
Define video content: Taping_____
Editing _____ Master tape _____ Second copy _____
Special effects additional cost: Dissolves _____ Freeze frames _____
Split screens _____ Audio dubbing _____ Mixing _____
Titles _____ Digital slides _____
Multiple camera capabilities _____
Delivery date of finished product _____
"Team" volunteer assistant _____ Phone _____
Business Name _____
Name of videographer assigned to your wedding _____
Address _____ Phone _____
Cost _____ Deposit _____ Payment schedule _____
Cancellation policy _____

Names of "must guests" to be photographed

Chapter 12

MUSIC:

Live Music:

Take time to think about music with special meaning for both of you: vocals, strings, keyboard, brass or woodwinds. If you have difficulty choosing from a vast selection of sacred or secular pieces, ask for assistance from friends, family, clergy or music librarian. Ask your clergy if there are guidelines for music that is acceptable for a wedding ceremony in the house of worship.

To locate musicians: ask friends for suggestions, contact your schools, college, universities, local orchestra and bands. Make it a point to hear the soloist or group yourself or ask for a demo tape. Indicate what you consider to be suitable attire for your event and an acceptable noise level. Consider booking your musicians for the ceremony and reception particularly if it all takes place in the garden. I found and booked a string quartet for my parents 50th wedding anniversary by phoning all the schools and colleges in the town where they lived. The musicians were first rate; some had played in the Montreal symphony. The afternoon reception held in my parents home in New York's Adirondack Mountains, was completely organized and set in motion from Canada where I lived at the time.

Disc Jockey

Disc Jockey's can provide entertainment and act as master of ceremonies, directing highlights of the reception as well as establishing sequence and timing of events. To find a DJ; consult your newspapers bridal supplement, radio stations or yellow pages.

Take note of the professionalism of the DJ when talking to him/her on the phone. Ask for a tape, video and literature. The personality of the DJ/master of ceremonies should match the effect you want to create at your party; sedate and dignified or upbeat and festive. Ask for and check referrals and Better Business rating.

Discuss your taste in music and ask for song lists and informational planning sheets. Keep in mind tunes that will appeal to a wide variety of tastes. Be sure that the DJ has professional equipment and not home consumer gear. Discuss suitable attire and an acceptable noise level.

CHECK LIST FOR MUSIC:

Live music:
Confirm that is your wedding date is available _____ Arrival time _____
Departure time _____ Hourly and overtime rates _____
Playing time _____Breaks _____
Dress code _____
Sound equipment provided _____Acceptable noise level _____
Music for special events: First dance _____Toasts _____
Blessing _____Cake cutting _____
Bouquet and garter toss _____Etc._____

       Musician   Instrument

_____
_____
_____

Company name _____
Address _____
Contact person _____ Phone _____
Total cost _____ Deposit _____ Payment schedule _____
Cancellation policy _____

Disc Jockey:
Confirm that your wedding date available _____ Time of arrival _____
Departure _____ Playing time _____ Breaks _____
Hourly rates _____ Overtime rates _____
Suitable attire: Describe _____
Song lists and informational planning sheets _____
Special song requests _____
Music for special events: First dance _____ Toasts _____
Blessing _____ Cake cutting _____
Bouquet and garter toss _____Etc._____
Is equipment professional standard? _____ Acceptable noise level _____
Business name _____
Disc jockey name _____
Address _____
Contact person _____ Phone _____

Notes for musicians and music selection

Chapter 13

FLOWERS

DO-IT-YOURSELF FLORAL ARRANGEMENTS:

If you plan to harvest and arrange your own blossoms, as Victorian ladies did, then the time of year your wedding is planned will dictate which flowers will come to your wedding. Enlist the support of friends and family for blooms from their gardens and pretty vases or pitchers. Check your yellow page listings for flower market or wholesale florists. Arts and craft stores are a must to visit for exploring supplies in do-it-yourself floral arrangements, bouquets and headpieces. Bouquet and centrepiece decorations, corsages and boutonniere of fresh, dried or silk flowers intermingled with herbs, carry symbolic meaning for your lives together. A bonus of dried or silk flower arrangements can decorate the home after your wedding.

Rosemary - remembrance	**Ivy** - fidelity , devotion
Marjoram - joy	**Mint** - warmhearted
Sage - prudence, honesty	**Parsley** - gaiety, enthusiasm
Wheat sheaves - prosperous and full life together	**Four leaf clover** - luck, opportunity

If you are landscaping your marital home, it makes good sense to decorate your garden wedding with flowering plants and shrubs before setting them in the garden. It makes even greater sense to stage the wedding ceremony and celebration in your lovely garden.

Tips On Keeping Flowers Fresh
1. Keep cut flowers in a cool place until ready to do the arrangement, then loosen bunched flowers and re-cut under water so stems draw in water, not air.
2. Keep flowers away from direct sunlight, heating or cooling vents and appliances.
3. Replace cloudy water and strip off leaves below water line.
4. Freshen bouquets, by sprinkling with water, placing in a plastic bag in a cool place.

Special Effects:
Fresh flowers worn in the hair as your headpiece is a beautiful effect. Fastened fresh, dried or silk flowers to combs, hair clip or head band. Braid the stems of fresh flowers into a lovely garland or secure flowers with fine wire. This is an alluring effect, recapturing the retro 1900 to 1940's look. Visit your local arts and craft store to see what is available. Chain stores such as Michaels and Ben Franklin have a fine selection and variety that will stimulate the creative process. To begin with, you will need a glue gun, and glue sticks. There are vials that hold water that keep fresh flowers perky. Attach one of these to a hair clip with a glue gun, and fill with water and a flower and spray of baby's breath. If you wear combs, headbands or hats you will find a wonderful assortment of decorative effects to use. Shop

around at stores that sell silk and dried flowers. The quality and detail in many artificial and dried flowers are quite lovely, life-like and true to the real thing. Combine flowers with: sequins, ribbons, glitter, nylon netting ,silk and beads to create exquisite effects. A plain hat can become many different new styles, as many as your imagination will grant.

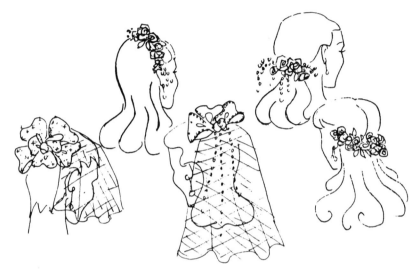

Butterflies:

Butterflies love flowers, so why not bring them to the wedding too. Imagine the ahhh's and oooh's when guests release from tiny boxes, live butterflies that ascend above the bride and groom the moment they say "I do." For more information, write: Insect Lore, Box 1535, Shafter, California 93263 or call (805) 746-6047.

Balloons

If you plan to decorate with balloons, arrange to have a "Team" member release several large clusters of pretty colored balloons at the moment you become man and wife. Keep the camera on alert for this spectacular lift-off. Combine multi colored balloons with flower arrangements. Tuck them in plants, shrubs and trees.

GARDEN CENTER/COMMERCIAL FLORIST:

Visit several florists that have been recommended to you by friends. Ask to see samples of the florists work and actual photos of recent weddings they have done. Discuss the style of your wedding: dress, theme, colors, and budget for flowers. The florist will be able to suggest arrangements and choice of flowers suitable for your wedding needs.

You can cut flower arrangement costs considerably if your ceremony and reception are in the garden. At a house of worship or chapel, be sure that the flowers can follow you to the reception site. Discuss this when booking the house of worship. In some cases they will insist that your flowers stay in the house of worship. When contracting the services of a florist, itemize every detail in your contract to avoid misunderstandings.

CHECK LIST FOR DO-IT-YOURSELF FLORAL ARRANGEMENT AND GARDEN CENTER/COMMERCIAL FLORIST

Do-It-For-Yourself Floral Arrangement:

	Variety	**Color**	**Source**	**Cost**
Brides bouquet				
Brides headpiece				
Attendants				
Groom				
Groom's men				
Mother of the bride				
Mother of the groom				
Ceremony				
Reception				

Equipment to decorate your wedding with flowers:

The following supplies are available at your local arts and craft supply stores.

glue gun_____ glue sticks_____ satin wired ribbon_____ silk _____

combs_____ hair clip_____ head band_____ beads_____ sequins_____

ribbons_____ glitter_____ bobbie pins_____ nylon netting _____

Surprise effects:

Butterfly ascent_____

Balloon lift-off_____

Garden Center or Commercial Florist:

Confirm that your wedding date is available _____ Delivery time _____

Will they set-up the floral arrangement? _____

Location for floral delivery _____

Floral arrangement instructions for:

	Variety	**Color**	**Arrangement**	**Cost**
Brides bouquet				
Brides Headpiece				
Attendants				
Groom				
Groomsmen				
Mother of the bride				
Mother of the groom				
Ceremony				
Reception				

Florist name _____

Address _____

Contact person _____ Phone _____

Cost _____ Deposit _____ Payment schedule _____

Cancellation Policy _____

Chapter 14

TRANSPORTATION

PERSONAL VEHICLES:

If personal vehicles are being used to take bride and groom to the ceremony and reception, assign a "Team" member driver(s) so that you can focus on events of the day. Plan your route so that you all arrive together. If transportation to and from the ceremony and reception presents a problem for some of your guests, particularly the elderly, you may want to organize car pools, or assign team members to pick up and deliver those beloved friends and family. Be sure "Team" drivers are reminded of their tasks just before the wedding.

HORSE, CARRIAGE AND COACHMAN:

One bridegroom surprised his equestrian bride by arranging for a horse drawn carriage to appear at the house of worship to take them on a leisurely ride to their garden reception site. The groom was handsomely dressed in a 19th century riding habit. When contracting this service be sure that your coachman is well-groomed and an experienced horseman that can handle emergencies (sudden sounds and excitable crowds). Inspect the carriage to be certain that it is clean and roadworthy and that the horse is also well groomed. Detail these points in your contract as well as date and time of arrival and departure and name and phone number of contact person. Include a tip for the coachman.

LEASED VEHICLES:

Vintage automobiles:
Weather on not you are a vintage car buff, this type of transportation can add the charm of an early 1900's quality to your wedding as well as provide transportation. Ask at your Chamber of Commerce, automobile dealerships or place a want ad in the newspaper for vintage cars. Be sure the automobiles are roadworthy (no break downs at this event), and clean. Have adequate insurance coverage.

Limousine:
A limousine can be leased to drive the bride and attendants to the house of worship and the wedding party to the reception site. Limousines can be leased on an hourly or flat rates. Include a tip for the driver. When leasing vehicles, do it a few months in advance, particularly during the busy wedding season. Be sure that you contract every detail: date and time of

pick up and delivery, or number of hours leased. Give clear directions or a map to destinations. Ask for the name and phone number of a contact person.

New Automobile leasing, Taxi service:

If you book well in advance or are a member of an automobile club special leasing rates on new automobiles are available for short or long term. Depending on the style of wedding you plan this may be a practical solution or an acceptable extravagance. Automobile leasing offers endless possibilities for your transportation requirements for the bride and groom, wedding party or out of town guests. An exotic automobile, a fun convertible or a sports utility van may be just what you need.

Taxi service in some areas offer unmarked luxury cars for transportation. With this arrangement you have a transportation when, where and for however long you need it, not to mention a professional driver.

CHECK LIST FOR TRANSPORTATION

Personal vehicles:
Confirm that vehicles are : Road worthy _____ Clean _____
Adequate liability and collision insurance coverage _____
Car pool "team" drivers and route plan:
Passenger _____ Phone _____ Pick up time_____
Address _____
"Team" driver _____
Passenger name _____ Phone _____ Pick up time _____
Address _____
"Team" driver _____
Passenger _____ Phone _____ Pick up time_____
Address _____
"Team" _____

Horse, Carriage and Coachman:
Confirm that your wedding date is available _____ Arrival time _____ Departure _____
Hourly rates _____ Overtime rates per hour _____
Experienced or coachman to handle emergency situations _____
Dress code for coachman _____ Is horse well groomed _____
Is carriage clean _____ and road worthy _____
Inclement weather clause _____
Adequate liability insurance coverage _____
Company name _____
Address _____
Contact person _____ Phone _____
Total cost _____ Deposit _____ Payment schedule _____

Leased vehicles: Vintage automobiles, Limousine, New Automobile and Taxi Service:
Confirm that your vehicle is available _____ Arrival/pick up time _____ Departure _____
Model _____ Color _____ Air conditioned _____
Rates: Hourly _____ Daily _____ Weekly _____
Overtime rates per hour _____ Driver _____
Liability insurance coverage _____
Company name _____
Address _____
Contact person _____ Phone _____
Cancellation policy _____

Chapter 15

CONCLUSION

It has been a joy to share *Bringing Home The Wedding Handbook* with you. I trust that it has been as beneficial for you as it has been for others. *Bringing Home The Wedding Handbook* will be expanded in the future. You are invited to participate in its development, by sharing your ideas, experiences, insights and recipes. Please take time to comment on your discoveries in planning your wedding and make suggestions in the form below. My sincere best wishes for love, joy and prosperity for you both in your journey through life together.

Bringing Home The Wedding
P. O. Box 782
Waynesville, NC 28786
Telephone: (828(452-7667)

Where did you hear about the handbook? _____

What sections were: Most beneficial _____ Least beneficial _____

List your wedding menu and include recipes _____

_____

Your personal discoveries and insights in planning your home and outdoor wedding _____

_____

_____

Can I quote comments you have made in the next edition? yes _____ no_____

signature _____ date _____

Enclose your wedding photos for possible use in the next edition and your signature for

permission for use Date: _____ Signature _____

Names of bride and groom _____

Address _____

City _____State _____ Zip_____

Phone (_____) _____ Wedding date _____ Number of guests _____

Location of wedding _____ Reception _____

Wedding vows _____ Toasts _____

Style of brides attire _____ Fabric_____ Color _____

Style of groom attire _____Fabric _____ Color _____

Additional information you wish to share:_____

_____

_____

_____

_____

EXCELLENT GIFT IDEA

Bringing Home The Wedding Handbook is an excellent gift for recently engaged couples. If you wish to order copies fill in one of the order forms below. Enclose check or money order for $24.95 plus $1.35 for shipping and handling. Please allow 7 to 10 days for delivery.

ORDER FORM:

Name_____

Address_____

Apartment #_____ PO Box_____

City_____State_____Zip_____

Phone (_____)_____Wedding date_____

Enclosed $_____Number of copies_____

Mail to: Bringing Home The Wedding Handbook
                     P. O. Box 782
                     Waynesville NC 28786

ORDER FORM:

Name_____

Address_____

Apartment #_____ PO Box_____

City_____State_____Zip_____

Phone_____Wedding date_____

Enclosed $_____ Number of copies_____

Mail to: Bringing Home the Wedding Handbook
                     P. O. Box 782
                     Waynesville NC 28786

BIBLIOGRAPHY

Dickson, Paul. *Toasts; The Complete Book of the Best Toasts, Sentiments, Blessings, Curses and Graces.* New York: Delacorte Press. 1988

Betty Crocker's Buffets. New York: Random House, Inc. 1984

Francois, La Perrier. *Wines, Spirits and Foods.* London, Canada: 1987

Field, Denise and Allan. *Bridal Bargains.* Bolder, CO: Windsor Peak Press 1996

Hynes, Angela. *The Pleasures of Afternoon Tea.* Los Angeles: HPBooks a division of Price Stern Sloan, Inc. 1987

Kaufman, William I. *The Coffee Cookbook.* Garden City New York: Doubleday & Company Inc.1964

Leviton, Richard. *Weddings By Design.* New York: HarperSanFrancisco A Division of HarperCollins Publishers. 1993

McCall's Introduction To French Cooking. New York: The McCall Publishing Company. 1971

Metrick, Sydney Barbara. *I Do.* Berkeley CA: Celestial Arts Publishing Company. 1992

Petrucelle, Don. *Poetic Odyssey.* Waynesville NC: 1996

Perry, Sara. *The Book of Herbal Teas.* San Francisco: Chronicle Books. 1997

Smith, Jeff. *The Frugal Gourmet Cooks With Wine.* New York: Avon Books A division of the Hearst Corporation. 1986

This handbook is dedicated
to you,

the Bride and Groom

May love light your home
and abundance fill your garden